# Lawrence Freedman

## The Revolution in Strategic Affairs

*Adelphi Paper* 318

Oxford University Press, Great Clarendon Street, Oxford OX2 6DP
Oxford New York
Athens Auckland Bangkok Bombay Calcutta Cape Town
Dar es Salaam Delhi Florence Hong Kong Istanbul Karachi
Kuala Lumpur Madras Madrid Melbourne Mexico City
Nairobi Paris Singapore Taipei Tokyo Toronto
and associated companies in
Berlin Ibadan

Oxford is a trade mark of Oxford University Press

Published in the United States
by Oxford University Press Inc., New York

© The International Institute for Strategic Studies 1998

**First published** April 1998 by **Oxford University Press** for
**The International Institute for Strategic Studies**
23 Tavistock Street, London WC2E 7NQ

**Director** John Chipman
**Editor** Gerald Segal
**Assistant Editor** Matthew Foley
**Design and Production** Mark Taylor

British Library Cataloguing in Publication Data
Data available

Library of Congress Cataloguing in Publication Data

ISBN 0-19-922369-6
ISSN 0567-932X

*contents*

After the end of the Cold War, the major Western states restructured their armed forces to take account of the sudden disappearance of the old threat and to meet the popular demand for a substantial 'peace dividend'. The cuts began before it was possible to get the measure of the post-Cold War world, which soon turned out to be a busier than expected place for armed forces. The restructuring process was combined with a number of military operations. These were widely spread around the world, including the Persian Gulf, the Balkans and Sub-Saharan Africa, and ranged from 'peace support' to armoured warfare.

The first round of cuts has now been made, and the peace dividend paid. Budgets and forces in the leading Western countries have been cut by anything from a third to a quarter of their Cold War size. Spending on procurement has fallen even more. Whether or not the new budgetary levels are sustainable, defence ministries are starting to pause for breath. They have an opportunity to think about the shape of armed forces over the longer term in the light of their experience of the 1990s.

The restructuring process has been drastic but not radical, with the essential features of the old order retained in the new. Land, sea and air are each the preserve of a distinctive service. Cooperation between the services, although no longer exceptional, is still thought a considerable achievement when it occurs. New equipment tends to improve on what has gone before and rarely represents a complete break with the past. As society has changed, so have the composition and culture of the forces, but there has been a lag. The same is true for organisational structures, which appear to be more hierarchical and rigid than those commonly found in the civilian sphere. To critics, this innate conservatism is intensely frustrating, out of line with the dynamic spirit of the times and out of touch with the likely character of future wars. It fails to grasp the full potential of what has come to be known as the 'revolution in military affairs' (RMA).

According to this revolution, a growing range of targets has become almost irredeemably exposed to attack by 'smart' weapons. The protection afforded by distance, size, terrain and weather has declined, a process accelerated through the application of information technology, here as elsewhere a dynamic and pervasive influence. As sensors and the means for data processing and its fusion and dissemination have improved, quite astonishingly so over the past decade, the full potential of weapons operating over long distances with precision guidance is closer to being realised. So extensive and constant are the flows of information that they can often only be tapped, rendered intelligible and acted upon by automatic processors. Human beings often seem barely to be involved: they simply do not have the processing capacity to cope.

The issues raised by these developments are not primarily of feasibility. With other ambitious ideas, such as President Ronald Reagan's Strategic Defense Initiative (SDI), the question of whether aspirations had leaped far ahead of technology, or even the laws of physics, was unavoidable. Not so in this case. Although the demands on software development and systems integration might have been underestimated, modern weapons clearly have a high probability of hitting targets when sent in the right direction with the right co-ordinates at the right time.

*'RMA' is the acronym of choice*

The RMA may now have become the 'acronym of choice in the US armed forces', attaining that status whereby all new developments must be rationalised in its terms, even though their origins lie elsewhere and their effects may be contradictory.[1] The RMA certainly covers a range of views. In some versions, it focuses largely on the conduct of major wars; in others, it influences all armed conflicts and might even be transforming the nature of conflict itself by opening up new sources of vulnerability and modes of attack. The RMA's most radical proponents see a disjuncture between the capacity of the technology and that of governments to appreciate and exploit it. They criticise a military establishment apparently ill at ease with such a profound challenge, especially when it requires a flatter command structure and a less parochial service outlook. For many, the basic revolution is not in the type of war nor the fundamentals of strategy, but in the excessively hierarchical and differentiated character of fighting forces.[2]

Sceptics worry that the enthusiasts forget the harsher – and constant – features of war that will continue to validate some of the more embedded elements of doctrine, training and forms of command. Claims that the 'fog of war' is about to be dispelled and that information can now serve as an independent weapon of war are treated with special caution. Other critics go further, noting that the debate on the RMA is being conducted largely within the military establishment, and that the motivation behind its promotion may be to sustain traditional notions of warfare against alternatives, in which the fearfulness of 'total war' and the confusion of terrorism and guerrilla warfare remain prominent.

## What Sort of Revolution?

The term 'revolution in military affairs' was first coined in connection with historical debates over the major changes in warfare that occurred in the sixteenth and seventeenth centuries. Later, it was used to refer to the impact of nuclear weapons. The term has advantages as a 'marketing device', dramatising issues by linking them to a sense of profound change, though at the risk of turning the idea of revolution into something hackneyed and without substance.

*Revolution* involves more than change, and certainly more than simply change of an incremental variety. It represents a moment of transformation. Such moments may not be appreciated until later historians study them; occasionally, they may be imagined in advance. With the RMA, as with most revolutions, there is confusion over whether it represents a stage in the historical process, or a vision that cannot be realised unless the visionaries seize the initiative. Will the revolution take place irrespective of efforts to help it on its way, or does it represent one set of objectives for policy which might be contradicted or qualified by others? As with political revolutions of the past, should this RMA be considered a single-step change, a movement to a new paradigm, or must it be a continuing process, a 'permanent revolution' that demands constant change? Can the revolution be confined to one country and still survive, or can it only take root if widely spread?[3]

This paper contends that a number of important changes are under way which, together, may indeed be revolutionary in their impact. But these changes do not necessarily point in one direction. Many of the technical advances associated with the RMA might be applied beneficially in a range of situations without producing anything approaching a transformation of warfare. The pure RMA may only be realised in very specific and quite unlikely circumstances.

Much of what is referred to under the RMA heading is the military expression of 'revolutions' in technological and business affairs. The revolution in technological affairs is the most profound and least contentious, and is founded on the bundle of activities associated with information technology, including sensors, computing and telecommunications. These activities have an evidently dynamic impact on decision-making and the efficient use of resources. This leads to the revolution in business affairs, encouraging companies to become much more adaptable, less hierarchical and ready to think in global terms. Not surprisingly, many of the companies said to exhibit these characteristics are also those engaged in the commercial exploitation of the new technologies. The RMA depends on their products, and they are often presented as a model to be followed in a military organisation. For this reason, many supporters of the RMA stress that they envisage something that involves organisational, as much as technical, changes.

One influential analysis detects a pattern whereby revolutions in military affairs occur through the interaction of technological change, systems development, operational innovation and organisational adaptation. These developments come together in a way that 'fundamentally alters the character and conduct of conflict'.[4]

This sort of analysis tends to play down the political and social dimensions of change, yet these can have a profound influence on military performance. The character and conduct of conflict must be influenced by who is fighting whom and over what. It is central to the argument of this paper that it is impossible to make sense of current trends without paying close attention to the impact of political change on military thought.

*Military Affairs* has broad connotations. It refers to the organisation and application of armed force on behalf of the state, so that a revolution might refer to major discontinuities in military means or political ends, or a combination of the two. The substantial changes in the international system over the past decade add to the list of revolutions one in political affairs. This is the consequence of the long-term effects of decolonisation combined with the short-term effects of the end of the Cold War and the growing impact of globalisation.

At the start of the 1990s, there was a brief flirtation with the concept of a 'fourth generation' of war, reflecting the decline of the old nation-state and traditional battle, and the irrelevance of traditional military forms and technologies to conflicts involving sub-state groups, such as ethnic militias and drug cartels.[5] As with Alvin and Heidi Tofflers' 'third wave' theory, which sees warfare adapting to the information age just as it did to the agricultural and industrial ages, attempts to produce schematic versions of history always seem to show the current moment as being one of fundamental transformation.[6] These approaches rarely withstand careful scrutiny.[7] This model did, however, at least have the virtue of asking questions about the impact of political rather than technical change on the conduct of war. In the new political setting, it appears less likely that major powers will go to war with one another, and more likely that they will find occasion to intervene in conflicts involving weak states. In these conflicts, the developments associated with the technical and organisational revolutions may not be so relevant. It is the tension between these two sets of tendencies that lies at the heart of this paper.

The link between the military and political spheres is the realm of strategy. If there is a revolution, it is one in strategic affairs, and is the result of significant changes in both the objectives in pursuit of which governments might want to use armed forces, and in the means that they might employ. Its most striking feature is its lack of a fixed form. The new circumstances and capabilities do not prescribe one strategy, but extend the range of strategies that might be followed. In this context, the issue behind the RMA is the ability of Western countries, and in particular the US, to follow a line geared to their own interests and capabilities.

## chapter 1

# A Western Way of War?

## The Essence of the RMA

The RMA depends on the interaction between systems that collect, process, fuse and communicate information and those that apply military force. The so-called 'system of systems' will make this interaction as smooth and continuous as possible.[1] As a result, military force will be directed in a decisive and lethal manner against an enemy still in the process of mobilising resources and developing plans. The vision is of a swift and unequivocal victory in war achieved with scant risk to troops, let alone the home population and territory.

In the elaboration of the RMA over the 1990s, the stress has been on the role of information in and around a battlefield – what has become known, reflecting a more multi-dimensional perspective, as the 'battlespace', the box, including breadth, width and height, within which a commander positions and moves forces over time. This is normally put at 40,000 square miles. The objective is to achieve 'Dominant Battlespace Knowledge', a capacity to process information in such a way that the overall operational environment, and the key relationships between the military units within it, can be described in as close to real time as possible. This will make possible a 'Near-Perfect Mission Assignment' and thus the use of 'Precision Violence'.

The growing importance of information flows is revealed in the jargon surrounding the RMA. Once, it was sufficient to talk of 'command and control' when referring to the methods by which responsible officers would receive news from their subordinates about the state of a battle and send back orders about what should be done next. Later, it became increasingly both possible and desirable to keep units in touch with one another across theatres of operation, while intelligence was arriving from specialised systems and not just those units in direct contact with the enemy. This led to the discussion of command, control, communications and intelligence ($C^3I$) as constituting a coherent set of problems. Now, defence analysts write about command, control, communications, computers, intelligence and battle management in the same vein. Although '$C^4I$/BM' is something of a mouthful, it conveys the view that information systems have become essential to an extremely wide – indeed comprehensive – range of functions and that they are also, in some critical sense, inter-dependent.

It is perhaps not surprising that the concept of the 'system of systems' was developed by an Admiral (William Owens). The US Navy's 'Co-operative Engagement Capability' integrates individual ship's radars to provide a single package of information available to all, pulling together units spread over thousands of miles into a coherent whole. At sea, as in the air, it may be possible to contemplate a battlespace empty of all but combatants. It has also always tended to be the case, even going back to the Second World War, that air and sea warfare have patterns susceptible to systematic analysis, which meant that the impact of technical innovations could be discerned. By contrast, land warfare has always been more complex, fluid and subject to a greater range of influences. Nonetheless, the aspiration for a 'system of systems' has also spread to ground forces. The US Army's Task Force XXI has been described as a 'digitized ground force' that will

> enhance situational awareness by providing accurate, complete, real-time information about friendly and enemy forces. The idea is to cut through the fog of battle to achieve information dominance over the enemy.[2]

For this reason, the most radical consequences of implementing the RMA would be felt by ground forces. The vision is remarkable. The ability to strike with precision over great distances means that time and space could become less serious constraints. Enemy units within the battlespace would be engaged from outside it. 'Smart' weapons are already less dependent on active manned guidance, and even on their ability to identify and chase the signatures of hostile systems. They are able to travel to specific co-ordinates that are updated as they travel. Targets will not need to be attacked in a sequential order of priority: there can be 'parallel warfare', as critical targets are attacked immediately and together.[3] 'Search and destroy' operations will become redundant if the enemy can be found electronically and destroyed from a distance. Ground forces may become little more than 'sensors', no longer needed to close with the enemy and seize territory. In order to stay agile and manoeuvrable, they will move with only that firepower required for self-defence, and will call in additional firepower from outside. Reliance on non-organic firepower will reduce dependence upon large, cumbersome, self-contained divisions and their associated potential for high casualties.

Traditional views of lines of command will need to be rethought:

> The new structure of warfare integrates and synchronises redundant, multiservice warfighting systems in simultaneous attacks on the enemy throughout his entire depth and in the space above him as well. All of this means that in future conflict the three levels of war, as separate and distinct loci of command and functional responsibilities, will be spaced and timed out of existence.[4]

If for each successful strike fewer and smaller munitions are needed, it becomes possible to envisage a much more austere transport infrastructure and reduced demands for storage of munitions and other consumables. As a result, 'heavy dependence upon ports, munitions depots and a large transport network' will decline.[5] Logistics demands can be eased further with a move to 'just-in-time warfare'. This would follow commercial practice, where delivery of goods 'just in time' cuts down on overheads, slack time and inventories. According to one analyst, better information should allow smaller

*the virtues of 'just-in-time' warfare*

amounts of lethal force to be provided quicker, thereby making possible a reduction in inventories and, as a result, less dependence upon potentially vulnerable logistical connections:

> *Just-in-time suggests that forces need no longer be massed prior to attack. When mass is needed for offensive or defensive purposes, it need take place only at the point of impact. Large formations of ships, planes or armor can give way to staggered scheduling and positioning that presents no discernible pattern to an adversary. Not being able to sense where the attack is coming from – because it could come from everywhere at any time – takes away the other side's initiatives. Putting the adversary on the defensive, reactive mode simplifies our problem and complicates his. It implies synchronising, planning, scheduling, ordering and delivering military operations as needed to meet currently emerging demands.*[6]

## A Western Way of War

This could be a prospectus for war that could pass muster at the Harvard Business School. It offers the efficient use of resources, based on splendid information, productive use of capital to get the best out of labour, and the contraction of distance. It also fits in with some long-standing Western preferences that have continually been reasserted during the twentieth century's encounter with 'total war'.

In the aftermath of the carnage of the First World War, military theorists such as Basil Liddell Hart attempted to develop an alternative approach to warfare. Liddell Hart wanted to limit the UK's liabilities to its allies, and its demands on its enemies, in the hope that this could prevent total war and mass slaughter. His model war would be fought by professional armies and based on manoeuvre more than attrition. Although he looked to new types of weapons, in particular the tank, to provide for fast-moving and decisive campaigns, Liddell Hart's claim was not so much that he was defining the way of the future, but reasserting constant principles of strategy (the 'indirect approach' intended to avoid the bloodiest encounters) and a long-established British way in warfare – designed to limit the UK's liabilities – from which the country had foolishly deviated in 1914–18.[7]

Yet the Second World War was even more 'total' than the First. In a book completed just after the Japanese surrender entitled *The Revolution in Warfare*, Liddell Hart saw no reason to change his mind on the folly of conceiving of war in terms of unlimited aims and unlimited methods, but acknowledged that the combination of the atomic bomb with aircraft and missiles able to bridge the gap between fighting zone and hinterland meant that, in practice, war was changing 'from a fight to a process of destruction'.[8]

The effort to reverse this tendency, so that war can again become a fight, is the core theme of much of the strategic theory of the past quarter-century, even in the nuclear sphere. The RMA represents the culmination of these efforts. It is important to recognise, however, that these efforts reflect Western, and more particularly US, aspirations which may not necessarily be shared by others. The rest of this chapter describes the key features of the developing Western Way of Warfare.

## Professionalism of Armed Forces

The professionalisation of their armed forces has not figured prominently in the current debate over the RMA in the UK and the US because both countries moved away from conscript armies some time ago. The stress on high-quality weaponry has reduced the relative importance of numbers, while at the same time putting a premium on high-quality troops. Conscripts are no longer needed as 'battle fodder'. Nor can they normally be trained to the level appropriate to modern warfare unless, as in Israel, society as a whole maintains itself at a high level of mobilisation. In addition, training young men and women inadequately to fight in unlikely wars is frustrating and alarming when a demand comes actually to fight. This became apparent to France during the Gulf War of 1991, when a reluctance to use conscripts left the country with remarkably few regular forces actually able to engage in combat.

## Intolerance of Casualties

Edward Luttwak has argued the need to reorganise armed forces to cope with a 'post-heroic' age. The expectations and beliefs that sustained a tolerance of casualties in earlier times are no longer present. Low birth-rates and smaller families make losses in combat even more unbearable, while there is a lack of the exaggerated nationalism that could sanction 'thousands of casualties in any minor military affray'.[9] All this puts a premium on framing strategies that keep casualties to a minimum. Whether popular attitudes are so fixed on this question is doubtful. It is by no means evident that thousands of casualties were ever tolerable in a minor affray, while for a conflict as serious as the Gulf War, preparations were made to cope with substantial coalition casualties, which fortunately did not arise. Nor is it self-evident that a lower value was put on human life in earlier times. The difference lay in circumstances and expectations. Nonetheless, the US Joint Chiefs of Staff have declared that 'In all cases, US military forces must be able to undertake operations rapidly, with a high probability of success, and with minimal risk of US casualties'.[10]

## Intolerance of Collateral Damage

The view that war is the responsibility of governments and armed forces but not the population at large leads to the presumption that all civilians must be deemed innocent unless proven guilty. This argues for targeting military assets rather than people. This is not only ethically much more acceptable, but also reflects the modern view that human beings are only as effective as the resources and technologies at their command allow. This morality interacts with the trend towards weapons of ever-greater precision, leading some to stress non-lethality, that is weapons that disable and contain rather than kill and that pose minimum long-term harm, either to combatants or to the environment.[11]

The concept of non-lethality is not in itself new (for example, tear-gas). Agents that temporarily disable or sticky substances that temporarily deny movement have obvious applications in either police or peacekeeping roles, but this is now being extended, almost as a prerequisite for any sort of legitimate force. Referring to the use of non-lethal weapons in Somalia, such as foams used to immobilise hostile civilians, US Colonel Martin Stanton saw these promising 'kinder, gentler operations other than war':

> We would like to see the development of nonlethal weapons
> as proof of our civility and restraint: nonlethal weapons show
> our reverence for life and our commitment to the use of
> minimal force.[12]

The series of developments that are brought together in the RMA have the connecting theme of the separation of the military from the civilian, of combatants from non-combatants, of fire from society, of organised violence from everyday life. As long as armed forces are organised around the Napoleonic belief in victory through decisive battle, it is natural to wish this to be achieved as quickly and as painlessly as possible, with the minimum of damage to civilian life and property. The alternative tendency – the hard battlefield slog, with casualties accumulating, treasury reserves depleted, industry pushed to full stretch and society becoming more fragile – is hardly appealing.

The advocates of strategic airpower and mechanised warfare after the First World War offered a strategy capable of producing a decisive and relatively pain-free victory. The Second World War demonstrated how exaggerated their claims had been. Further confirmation of the apparent hopelessness of any attempt to contain war within acceptable limits was provided by the arrival of nuclear weapons in 1945. This suggested that the search for a route to a decisive battle was over. If the grim tendency towards total war could not be opposed by preparing to fight a limited war, perhaps it could be countered by making its 'deadly logic' inescapable. Preparing for a war that was likely to end in utter catastrophe pushed the logic to the extremes, so that war's initiation moved out of the realm of rational policy.

## chapter 2

# The Origins of the RMA

## The Nuclear RMA

Soviet theorists described the impact of nuclear weapons as a 'revolution in military–technical affairs'.[1] The mass-production of hydrogen bombs gave this revolution an extreme form. For NATO countries, nuclear deterrence offered a relatively inexpensive way of convincing the Soviet Union that it would be foolish to attempt to change the international status quo by any military means, even though the US was unable to sustain its advantage in the nuclear sphere.

The US military clung to the hope that new missile and anti-missile technology would allow it to turn a nuclear war into a quest for a meaningful victory, rather than a descent into vicious, calamitous and purposeless exchanges of megatonnage. By the mid-1960s, this quest looked futile. Hence, the proclamation of the condition of 'mutual assured destruction'. In the absence of a decisive asymmetry, a nuclear symmetry – the 'strategic balance' – seemed to be the next best thing, so much so that the two superpowers worked hard, with modest success, to find ways of codifying this symmetry in a mutually acceptable form through arms-control negotiations. The idea of 'balance' might have been misleading, hiding a range of divergences in strategic culture, capabilities and doctrine, but suggested routes to a nuclear victory appeared even less compelling.

Nuclear deterrence worked better in practice than in theory. It was barely tolerable as a grand strategy, overhung as it was by the nagging question: 'what happens if deterrence fails?'. In case the exigencies of the moment demanded an answer to that question, the search had to continue – though without much confidence – for a more contained form of warfare.

This did not necessarily preclude nuclear use. In the 1950s, schemes for limited nuclear war were devised, but failed to convince because of the destructiveness and irradiation caused by even a small nuclear weapon and the expectation of swift escalation to total war. In the 1970s, these ideas started to be revived, but with new technologies rendering the weapons more accurate over longer ranges, and so more discriminating in use and susceptible to effective central control.

Out of this effort developed many of the systems now associated with the conventional RMA, including work on miniaturisation, precision guidance and propulsion technology. These developments came together to produce the long-range cruise missile, one of the most important military innovations of the 1970s, which was understood at the time to be blurring the lines between conventional and nuclear capabilities.[2] Also of great importance was the development of a space-based infrastructure, with specialist satellites geared to reconnaissance, geodesy, meteorology and data-relay. In 1983, Reagan launched his SDI, which was in part inspired by the possibility that space-based systems might be able to intercept ballistic missiles soon after their launch. While this effort was designed to reduce the nuclear threat, its most significant long-term effects were probably in the boost it gave to technologies with more conventional military applications.

A credible means of fighting a nuclear war was not found because of the inherent problems of conducting complex military engagements in nuclear conditions and the likelihood that, however discriminating the initial nuclear strikes, their unavoidable collateral damage would lead to escalation to all-out devastation. The alternative approach was to find ways of prolonging the conventional phase of a war to provide an opportunity for diplomacy to prevent further escalation.

Conventional strategy became more important to both NATO and the Warsaw Pact during the late 1960s.[3] Given the assumed (and exaggerated) Eastern quantitative superiority in conventional forces, NATO was always on the look-out for qualitative improvements as 'force multipliers'. In this context, military planners borrowed concepts developed in the course of the vain attempt to generate decisive and discriminating nuclear strikes and began to apply them to conventional operations, along with many of the technologies that supported them.[4]

## Emerging Technologies

The technologies developed in an effort to refine nuclear strategy had obvious applications from the start in conventional operations. Satellites were in use for reconnaissance purposes by 1961 and for communications (in Vietnam) in 1965. The first tactical computers were used in 1966. The Internet can be traced back to a Pentagon-backed project to link together computers in the 1960s. The first e-mail message was sent in 1972. The first demonstration of the potential of modern missiles is often said to be the Egyptian Navy's attack on the Israeli ship *Eilat* using *Styx* anti-ship missiles in October 1967. Evidence of the potential impact of 'smart' weaponry came with its use during the US Air Force (USAF)'s *Linebacker* campaigns in the closing stages of US military involvement in the Vietnam War.[5] Confidence that the trend could include moving as well as fixed targets was reinforced by the success of air-defence and anti-tank weapons during the opening stages of the October 1973 Arab–Israeli War.

Most of the core technologies now associated with the RMA could be listed by the early 1970s: precision guidance; remote guidance and control; munitions improvements; target identification and acquisition; command, control and communications; and electronic warfare.[6] The agenda included the lethality of attacking weapons, the

*core RMA technologies appeared in the 1970s*

range from which they could be fired without loss of accuracy, the quality of the information on both the enemy target-set and one's own forces, and the speed with which these could be related to each other. The most modern weapons were becoming dependent on electronic systems to track and attack enemy targets, and also to prevent the enemy from tracking and targeting them. Thus, the technological trend has been evolutionary, rather than revolutionary.

As early as 1974, Dr Malcolm Currie, then Director of Defense Research and Engineering, testified to Congress that a 'remarkable series of technological developments have brought us to the threshold of what will become a true revolution in conventional warfare'.[7] A decade later, US Secretary of Defense Caspar Weinberger was also referring to technology 'revolutionizing the conventional battlefield'.[8] The theme, therefore, like the technology, is not new.

In 1985, Seymour Deitchman, then Vice-President for Programs at the Institute for Defense Analysis, observed, in terms that have since become commonplace, that:

> *We are in the midst of a period of revolutionary change in the technology of the general purpose military forces ... Over the next decade or two, those forces will be transformed radically in their doctrines, modes of operation, and capabilities ... The revolution in military affairs is driven by the same technological advances that are making startling changes in the civilian world. These advances include mainly the application of solid-state electronics to computation, sensing, guidance, communication, and control of all manner of devices and machines.*

Deitchman even referred to improvements in sensing, electronic warfare and command, control and communications as bringing the 'information war' to the fore as 'a primary rather than an ancillary part of direct conflict'.[9]

Why did this 'revolution in military affairs' not catch on in the 1980s as it did in the subsequent decade? The answer lies not only in the maturity of the relevant systems or in the ability of military organisations to think imaginatively, but also in the political setting. The debate on the future of conventional forces was, in the 1980s, still shaped by the prospect of a NATO–Warsaw Pact encounter on the Central Front. Each alliance possessed formidable conventional capabilities, developed out of those that had been used in earlier wars in the same part of the world, and each could call on great nuclear arsenals.

Analysis of the implications of new technologies could not just be an exercise in futurology. It had to be part of the constant effort to sustain a military balance in the light of actual and prospective Soviet capabilities. Here, quantity mattered as much as quality. The potential enemy's numerical strength had to be addressed, especially when it could not be assumed that the qualitative difference was large. The nuclear dimension meant that any conventional breakthrough might do no more than trigger a nuclear riposte. Meanwhile, the demands of alliance meant that the location and visibility of forces were often more important than their actual value in combat. From this perspective, analyses such as Deitchman's could be challenged by three different groups: the US military, the allies and the reformers.

## The Military Critique

The real target of Deitchman's essay was the balance of priorities in the defence budget. His concern was that systems once designated as being merely for 'support' were becoming as important, and as expensive, as ships, aircraft and armoured fighting vehicles: 'These systems are coming, in many respects, to usurp the platforms' claim to be the real basis of military power'. Continuing with the established institutional biases, Deitchman warned, would result in the development of a remarkable ability to move forces over long distances 'without having effective combat capability at the end of the line'. These biases, he suggested, reflected the unwanted degree of integration that systems implied among the services.

The military was wary about treating aircraft, ships and tanks as no more than 'launching systems', and in this it enjoyed considerable industrial and legislative backing. It was not, however, only a matter of superior political muscle. The military recognised the importance of advanced weapons and systems to warn of an attack, divert an incoming missile and offer serious and sustainable target acquisition. It also recognised the intensive research and development effort this required.

Yet without platforms nothing could be carried and there would be no force to be 'multiplied'. If these multipliers proved to be vulnerable to enemy counter-measures then they could also turn out to be force dividers, leaving units blinded and isolated. The multiplication effect itself was not proven until there was more clarity on how these new capabilities would come together in practice. Individually, many of the 'smart' weapons were too expensive to be expended in regular, large-scale and realistic exercises. The role of the new technologies in war-fighting was hard to prove. Most important, so long as the starting-point for the political measurement of military power was platforms, then they would be privileged in the defence budget.

## The Allies' Critique

West European governments tended to view all US proposals for enhancing conventional capabilities with suspicion. They had little slack in their defence budgets and were wary of attempts to commit them to expensive new systems. Their basic inclination was to rely on nuclear deterrence, which seemed to have worked perfectly well in producing a stable relationship with the Soviet bloc, and saw little reason to move to a new doctrine. At worst, proposals for new conventional technologies appeared as alibis for US disengagement.

The rise of the anti-nuclear movement of the late 1970s and early 1980s did argue for reduced dependence upon nuclear weapons by means of conventional 'deep-strike' substitutes for the more 'tactical' missions.[10] Weinberger proposed an Emerging Technology Initiative at the Bonn NATO summit in June 1982. This prompted the standard European concerns. While the exact cost of these proposals was disputed, the pressure on defence budgets already allowed scant room for manoeuvre. There were suspicions that the basic objective was to drum up new business for US defence contractors.[11] Not surprisingly, the position was summed up most starkly by a leading French official, Henri Conze, who told the 1984 IISS conference that:

> I do not believe that it is in our interest to let anybody think that a short-term technical revolution could drastically change the military balance between the two Blocs. Nor will new conventional weapons technology permit us to relax our efforts in the nuclear field. If those two propositions are not clearly perceived, I am convinced that the gains in prospect from the new technologies would turn out to be negative.[12]

## The Military Reform Movement

The new technologies also failed to enthuse those Americans who were considered to be among the most innovative strategic thinkers of the time, such as Steven Canby, William Lind and Edward

Luttwak.[13] Described as military reformers, but not revolutionaries, they produced a scathing indictment of the status quo. Leadership in the armed forces, they alleged, had become devoted to the management of procurement and the most prized skills had become bureaucratic ones. This led to a loss of strategic imagination, reflected in a readiness to persist with attrition in war, aiming to wear down the enemy in a slugging match. The reformers wanted instead to revive the traditional arts of the General, and to move towards a strategy that could exploit them. They were particularly concerned with what they perceived to be the more sophisticated Soviet grasp of what was described as the 'operational art'.[14] Their views pointed to rapid movement of forces as the means by which decisive outcomes could be produced in a land war.

Many of the reformers' ideas fitted in with the determination of the US military to reconstruct itself after Vietnam by improving its own grasp of the principles of military strategy as well as through the continued exploitation of the country's technological strength. This philosophy would be manifest in a move towards a greater reliance on manoeuvre, much more demanding operationally but much more rewarding in combat and potentially far less costly in casualties. Its high point came in 1982, when the revised version of the US

*the risks of looking at technology in isolation*

Army Field Manual was said to have incorporated many of the ideas of the reformers, and the 'AirLand Battle' concept was in vogue, although it was also widely believed that references to manoeuvre warfare were essentially sops to a politically influential philosophy, rather than an embrace of it.[15] The influence of the reformers' ideas can still be felt in current definitions of the 'operational art' as helping

> commanders understand the conditions for victory before seeking battle, thus avoiding unnecessary battles. Without operational art, war would be a set of disconnected engagements, with relative attrition the only measure of success or failure.[16]

The reform movement in turn attracted considerable criticism as offering an essentially romantic and nostalgic view of the strategic art, unhampered by the normal constraints of politics and economics, and as being over-impressed by Soviet doctrine and procurement practices. The reformers were said to exaggerate Soviet vulnerability to manoeuvre warfare, as well as the Western ability to implement it successfully. Implementation of their proposals on NATO's Central Front would, if anything, increase the risk of terrible casualties and a Soviet breakthrough.[17] Critics also considered naïve the belief that strategy could shape technology. Yet they also tended to acknowledge that an exaggerated confidence in technology could be to the detriment of US forces.

The reformers were opposed to the view that developments in conventional technology favoured the defence, or that technical 'fixes' could be an alternative to doctrinal innovation. As the equipment component of the defence budget supported progressively fewer systems, the budget as a whole would support progressively fewer combat troops. Equipment was becoming unnecessarily complicated as it reached out for new capabilities well beyond the point of diminishing marginal returns.[18] This equipment was difficult to maintain, unreliable and required putting even more resources into the logistics 'tail', with complicated procurement processes that meant that it entered service long after new generations of Soviet equipment. Soviet equipment, by contrast, was simpler, more robust, affordable in large numbers and suitable for an army on the move.

According to Lind, whatever the high theoretical probabilities of kill offered by the new systems, in practice they achieved far less. Terrain, weather, dust, smoke and enemy tactics all created problems of target identification. These were compounded when those operating the systems, often fearful of their own vulnerability, lacked the time or the regular opportunities to use them efficiently. Instead of making the individual soldier's life simpler, the new technology threatened to make it more complex. Looking at technology in isolation, Lind cautioned, 'is a prescription for [the] failure to create a self-reinforcing tactical system, or for the breakdown of an existing one'. The term revolution, he observed, 'should not be trivialised', but should define 'a dialectically qualitative change in the art of war'. Lind did not believe that there had been such a change in conventional warfare since the Second World War.[19] According to Canby:

> *New technologies will obviously change the* techniques *by*
> *which things are done in war, but they will change neither*
> *the* nature *of these things (e.g., gathering intelligence,*
> *commanding, striking, protecting and moving about) nor the*
> principles *according to which these things are done*
> *(surprise, concentration, economy of forces, security, etc.).*[20]

The major NATO proposal of the early 1980s was concerned with deep strikes to the enemy rear, against fixed targets, such as bridges or airfields, and so played to the new technology's known strengths. There was far more scepticism about being able to track and attack with much accuracy anything on the move. Moreover, as Canby noted:

> *As the scale descends from equipment-oriented and formal*
> *warfare to light-infantry and guerrilla warfare, especially in*
> *close terrain, increasing importance must be given to such*
> *intangibles as uncertainty, surprise, training, tactics, adapt-*
> *ability, national characteristics and the like.*[21]

## The Soviet Perspective

Given the institutional biases in the West towards a cautious appreciation of the new technologies, it is perhaps not surprising that their potential impact was appreciated more in the East. Soviet planners were painfully aware of their country's deficiencies in advanced technology, especially in electronics, and sensed that the US was gaining a significant qualitative advantage.

Soviet military leaders, wishing to warn their political masters about the dangers of falling further behind, were therefore the first to proclaim, in the early 1980s, a new military–technical revolution.[22] Marshal-General Nikolai Ogarkov in particular fretted about the capacity of the US to develop 'reconnaissance-strike complexes' that would enable commanders to detect targets and then attack at long ranges. At the time, Western analysts were still mainly concerned with assessing the state of Soviet opinion on the nuclear, rather than the conventional, balance.

This developing Soviet concern became much clearer in retrospect. For example, as John Holdren observed in 1987, an important motive for the Soviet campaign against SDI was fear that it was 'an invitation to an expensive, head-to-head technological competition in an arena where US advantages in sensors, high-speed computing, pointing and tracking, and so on give the United States a formidable edge'.[23]

## The Impact of the Gulf War

Until 1990, there was a lack of hard evidence as to how the new technologies might work in practice. There had only been indications of what they might achieve, for example their use by Israel in Lebanon's Bekaa Valley in 1982 and in the Falklands campaign of the same year. Although the 1980s saw much armed conflict, some on a substantial scale, the belligerents had only limited access to the most advanced types of weapons. The US had little scope to test AirLand Battle-type theories. In general, the enemies faced – hostage-takers in Iran, snipers in Grenada, car-bombers in Lebanon, drug-traffickers in Panama – did not require the implementation of the more ambitious battle-plans.

The collapse of European communism at the end of 1989 meant that the US was suddenly left as the world's sole superpower. Proposals for new conventional capabilities would no longer need to be assessed by reference to NATO's Central Front, and could be expected to extend US advantages rather than ease its weaknesses. The sense of ultimate dependence upon nuclear threats was lessened dramatically. Military planners had an unusual opportunity to engage in fresh thinking about the future of armed conflict. In August 1990, just as this was getting under way, Iraq invaded Kuwait. The crisis proved resistant to diplomatic remedies and was only eventually resolved through a major war.

*the war was a revolution of expectations*

The Gulf War transformed perceptions of US conventional strength. Up to this point, confidence in the capacity of the US armed forces to wage war effectively was not high. On the eve of *Operation Desert Storm*, there was a widespread presumption that coalition forces could suffer badly in any move against a well-entrenched Iraqi defence precisely because they had become over-dependent upon advanced military technology. The talk was of likely mistakes, as the desert sand would interfere with delicate equipment and malfunctioning indicators would lead coalition units to inflict as much damage on each other as on the enemy. It was almost taken for granted that casualties on any significant scale would be too much for the US political system to bear and would oblige President George Bush to accept an inconclusive settlement. These negative expectations, which may well have encouraged Iraqi President Saddam Hussein to risk a war with the US, underestimated the seriousness with which the US military leadership had addressed the deficiencies exhibited in Vietnam and embraced the promise offered by the new technologies. First and foremost, therefore, the revolution resulting from the Gulf War was one of expectations. Up to 1991, the US seemed to have lost its grip on the art of warfare; after *Desert Storm*, it appeared unbeatable – at least when fighting on its own terms. The war also provided verisimilitude and credibility to what might otherwise have appeared as professional musings based on extravagant technical claims.

Because the Gulf War was so one-sided, it provided an opportunity to display in a most flattering light the potential of modern military systems. It was as if Saddam had been asked to organise his forces in such a way as to offer coalition countries the opportunity to show off their forces to their best advantage. A battle-plan unfolded that followed the essential principles of Western military practice against a totally outclassed and out-gunned enemy which had conceded command of the air. There were no chronic deficiencies in either resources or logistics, apart from some unseasonable weather. The result, as noted in the *Gulf War Air Power Survey*, was not 'merely ... a conducive environment for the successful application of Western-style air power' but 'circumstances ... so ideal as to approach being the best that could be reasonably hoped for in any future conflict'.[24] This limited the extent to which formal doctrines, staff training, procurement policies and so on could be deemed validated.

Iraqi strength had been seriously overestimated as a result of successes in a very different sort of conflict – with Iran in 1980–88 – and through a focus on its quantities of manpower, tanks and aircraft. The quality of the equipment was in some cases more than respectable, but the Iraqi military leadership had been purged regularly lest it develop political aspirations, many of the best troops (in the Republican Guard) had been held back to protect the regime, and the bulk of the forward troops were conscripts. The US, British and French forces participating in *Desert Storm* were professionals. In addition to superior training, they also enjoyed great advantages in overall firepower. This was marked at sea, but most significant in the air.

In the Gulf, advanced technology was employed to fight an essentially classical conventional campaign to a swift and decisive conclusion and with limited casualties (especially on the coalition side). There was a compelling demonstration of precision guidance – most dramatically in the images of 'smart' bombs entering a command centre, or of a *Tomahawk* cruise missile, fired 1,000 kilometres away from an old battleship converted for the purpose, navigating its way through the streets of Baghdad, entering its target by the front door and then exploding. Targets were – generally – chosen with care and – generally – attacked with confidence and a minimum of collateral damage.

While the intelligence picture was by no means complete, it was significantly better than that available to commanders in previous wars. The quality of communications was also impressive. As well as the first 'information war', *Desert Storm* has been proclaimed as the world's first 'space war', although no battles took place in space and no shots were fired from space.[25] Sixty-four individual satellites, of 23 different types, were available to the coalition when Kuwait was invaded. They were largely American and quite a number, available for communications, meteorology and some imagery, were civilian.[26] At each stage, space-based systems provided not only intelligence, but also told individual units where they were, what forces they faced and what their commanders thought they should do. Information from space brought units together when cooperation was required, and kept them apart when collision was feared. It warned of imminent attacks and changes in the weather. Space-based systems identified targets, worked out their co-ordinates, helped to choose the weapons system best placed to attack them, passed on the orders to attack, provided mid-course corrections to ensure accuracy and then checked afterwards to ensure that everything had gone according to plan.

There was a surge in the distribution of satellite terminals. These moved with the forces – and for that matter their media-camp followers – ensuring that everyone was constantly in touch with everyone else. One system apparently critical to the coalition's ability to execute complex manoeuvres in the desert or operate efficiently at sea was the *NAVSTAR* Global Positioning System (GPS), whose quality appeared as something of a revelation, leading to a great demand for receivers. It released coalition units from needing to worry about visibility or landmarks when working out their location. Before this conflict, *NAVSTAR*'s importance had not been appreciated, even by the military. Now it had 'come of age'.[27] By contrast, the Iraqis appeared to have been rendered blind, deaf and dumb. Iraq might have been moving towards the launch of its own satellites (with the *Tamouz* launcher) but had yet to achieve this. Iraq used commercial systems for communications, but these were not resistant to jamming. Their own means of jamming tended to reveal the locations of the units involved. Some GPS receivers, which had been used in oil exploration, were available, but these had not been integrated into military systems.

The overall impression was misleading. Many more 'dumb' than 'smart' bombs were used and, in one of the more misrepresented exchanges of the war, a supposedly 'smart' defensive missile (the *Patriot*) failed to cope with an extremely 'dumb' offensive one (the *Scud*).[28] Appropriate targets were not always found, nor destroyed when they were, and 'collateral damage' was not always avoided. Satellites were not the only sensors or the only means of communication. In practice, the fusion of communications and sensor data, which many would see as the essence of 'information warfare', was by no means complete, and seems to have been improvised in many respects, leaving important deficiencies.[29] Certainly, the 'fog of war' was not lifted; rather, it took on new forms.[30]

Although deficiencies were apparent, it did not take much imagination or leaps of technological fancy to see how this form of warfare could be taken further. It left no doubt about the importance of air power. Although some exaggerated claims led to a largely futile post-war debate in the US on the relative contributions of air and land forces to *Desert Storm*, it is hard to avoid the conclusion that, while the coalition's armies were vital to securing victory, their task had been made much easier by the attrition, disorientation and loss of will imposed on Iraqi forces through sustained air attacks.[31] The opening hours mocked the massive Iraqi investment in active air defences.

If the Iraqis had no answer to air power, future opponents could be expected to fare even worse, whatever the quality of their available manpower and firepower, because the US could now begin to take full advantage of the new possibilities for intelligence, command, control, communications, surveillance and damage assessment. It was not hard to sketch out a rosy future for the US armed forces, in which they might expect to be able to dominate any adversaries in battle.

This led to the launch of the RMA, initially described, in a term borrowed from the Russians, as a 'Military–Technical Revolution' (MTR). Andrew Marshall, the long-standing head of net assessment at the Pentagon, had been sponsoring studies of these developments for some time and seized the chance to dramatise their potential. US Secretary of Defense Richard Cheney referred to a revolution in the immediate aftermath of the war, claiming that its possibilities had just been 'demonstrated dramatically'.[32] One academic study concluded after the war that, although the revolution was still under way, 'its outlines have become clear'.[33] The language soon shifted to a stress on RMA rather than MTR in order to avoid putting technology at the centre.[34]

*the Gulf War launched the RMA*

Although the revolution was phrased in technical and organisational terms, most critical was the change in the political context. The end of the Cold War meant that the old limits on conventional innovation had been relaxed, and were no longer constrained by a scenario dominated by an extremely strong opponent, enjoying significant logistical advantages, in a conflict with a predisposition to 'go nuclear' at any time. Military planners could prepare to fight a war as they would like it to be fought, and showed what they could do in the Gulf. This appeared to validate a particular line of technological and doctrinal development. Whether or not this presaged a revolution in military affairs depended on whether future patterns of conflict would offer similar opportunities.

## chapter 3

# Asymmetric Wars

Without the 'threat' of Soviet-sponsored aggression, Western governments became as preoccupied with the problem of whom they were likely to fight as how they would do so. With no clear lines to follow, long-term planning tended to reflect the preoccupations and priorities of the moment by extrapolating from current points of tension. Discussion of potential enemies rarely extended beyond naming the obvious candidates with whom relations were currently poor. Thus, the US set itself a standard of being able to fight a war in East Asia and one in the Middle East simultaneously.

Although much American military literature refers to 'peer competitors', with comparable military endowments to those of the US, it is not so easy to work out exactly who these might be. Historically, there have rarely been many candidates for such a role. Scenarios involving the Germans and the Japanese remain fanciful, despite the best efforts of some novelists and the occasional international-relations theorist. Russia is in no fit state to regain the empire it has just relinquished. China is more self-confident and inclined to flex its muscles in regional disputes, but is not positioning itself to disrupt the whole international order, and lacks the strength to mount substantial military operations in its own region. Alternatively, for those who wish to stretch their imaginations, there have been prognostications of a 'clash of civilisations'[1] or some all-consuming anarchy,[2] but these remain highly contested.

The best prognosis is that conflicts will continue to be regionally confined, sometimes reflecting deliberate power-plays by local revisionists, but more often arising from within weak states – countries caught on the margins of the global economy, released from colonial rule but suffering from compound social fractures that cannot be healed when resources are scarce and political institutions feeble. The range of future problems of this nature may depend on the success of efforts to cope with those that are already manifest. A key factor may be overall economic health. A relaxed view about conflict in and around East Asia, for example, has been closely correlated with optimism about the dynamism of the local economies. With that optimism badly dented, some regimes may feel more insecure and have a heightened sensitivity to local tensions and rivalries.

Despite all the uncertainty, it can be assumed that, for the foreseeable future, no other state will be able to match the conventional military strength of the US, even before the addition of that of its main allies. Consideration of future war, therefore, has to distinguish between conflicts in which the US will be involved, and those in which it will not. The second type allows for a great variety of combinations of belligerents. The first type has a built-in asymmetry because the US will always be superior militarily to its opponents.

The political ambitions of the US and the other major Western powers do not depend on regular exertions of preponderant military power. They do not seek to change the status quo by force, but only to respond to the efforts of others to do so. Even then, discretion is retained over when and how to respond. Hence, the mixed picture of involvement in regional conflicts, with tentative or inappropriate responses to the tragedies in Algeria or the African Great Lakes region. For the moment, war is more a matter of choice than of necessity.

*the West sees war as a choice, not a necessity*

The asymmetry in capabilities goes in one direction; the asymmetry in interests goes in another. For the US and its allies, this critical asymmetry of interests might be so sharp that they will see no purposes served by becoming involved and good reasons to keep clear: the intractability of the conflicts; their brutalising impact on all involved; the capacity of outsiders to make things worse rather than better; the ease of entry compared with that of exit. Yet not all conflicts can be viewed with disinterest. If a conflict is close to home, there is a risk that its effects will be felt within Western societies. There are good reasons to be wary of situations that allow gangsters and drug-traffickers to flourish, prompt extremists to export violence or encourage local bullies and predators. Substantial population movements, collapsing local currencies, disrupted markets and sources of important commodities such as oil can all have substantial knock-on effects. Images of human distress on a massive scale and violations of human rights can prick Western consciences and discredit passivity. If non-military remedies such as diplomatic missions and economic sanctions are inadequate, the calculable losses of intervention can be outweighed by the less calculable damage resulting from non-intervention.

During the Cold War, decisions on intervention tended to be influenced by core strategic imperatives. The experience of the unfortunate multinational force in Beirut in 1983–84 led to an important debate in the higher reaches of the Reagan administration over the conditions under which future military interventions should be contemplated. Weinberger set out six tests before US combat forces should be used abroad: the engagement is vital to the national interest; the intention is to win; objectives must be clear; if objectives change, so must combat requirements; some assurance of popular and Congressional support; and the action should be a last resort. Secretary of State George Shultz warned that, as a major power, the US could not fight only the 'fun wars'.[3]

In 1993, President Bill Clinton proposed comparable questions to be asked of a peacekeeping operation. Was there: a clear threat to international peace? A clear objective? An identified exit point? How much will it cost?[4] General Colin Powell, when Chairman of the Joint Chiefs of Staff, had already made known his cautious answers to such questions. He distrusted 'constabulary duties', preferring that the US role be confined to dealing with the most serious challenges to national security and international order.[5]

## Stability Support or Rule Enforcement?

Will the asymmetries in military power favouring the West compensate for those in interests that might tend to isolationism? Only if the available military power is appropriate to the relevant contingencies and objectives. In terms of objectives, it is possible to distinguish between *rule enforcement* – ensuring that all states behave according to the dictates of a stable, civilised and just international society; and *stability support* – bringing some sort of order to a troubled part of the world. In terms of contingencies, it can be assumed that violence has already been introduced (or appears about to be introduced) by others.

Stability support requires working with local political forces in order to calm relations between them and develop opportunities for constructive action. For this reason, operations of this nature have been seen to require the consent of the parties involved. Rule-enforcement operations, by contrast, are likely to arise in response to a blatant violation of some international law or norm. The objective will be to reverse the offending action, either through the direct application of force, or else through a coercive threat. In practice, the operational requirements may not be that distinct.

Stability support based on consent, as in traditional peacekeeping, is only usually possible after a cease-fire. As was discovered in Bosnia-Herzegovina, a consensual operation is almost impossible to establish prior to a cease-fire because of the constant shifts in the circumstances of the warring parties which force them to reassess the bases for earlier consent. Actions of an avowedly humanitarian nature, such as delivering food and medical supplies to a besieged city, can be seen as hostile.

With rule enforcement, the basic rule is non-aggression, which suggests either deployments to deter armed invasion or operations along the lines of *Desert Storm* to reverse any initial gains. But, if the norms being enforced are connected with minority or human rights, reflecting contemporary concerns about ethnic conflict and repressive regimes, rule enforcement may require acting on behalf of the victims in a great range of situations.

The experience of the 1990s suggests that it may be difficult to have rule enforcement without stability support. The after-shocks of military action mean that it is difficult for an intervening power to walk away from the consequences of intervention. In the case of Iraq, for example, this meant accepting some responsibility for the fate of the Kurdish people. In Bosnia, once the Serbs had agreed to cooperate with the diplomatic effort that led to the 1995 General Framework Agreement for Peace in Bosnia and Herzegovina (the

Dayton Accords), stability-support questions came to the fore once more, as reflected in the designation of the follow-on to the original Intervention Force (IFOR) as a Stabilisation Force (SFOR). Any external interference, whether in setting rules for the conduct of the conflict, easing suffering, brokering a settlement, or intervening on one side, will influence the balance of power. When it ceases, there will always be a tendency for the local factors to dominate the play once again. Thus, intervention is not so much directed against a specific end, but is rather a part of a process. The role of force lies in coercion or in the construction of areas of political support and the erosion of those of opponents. These are matters in which patience is a virtue.

Assembling a coalition in order to intervene can be a politically complex process. Even if able to act unilaterally, most states prefer to act as part of a coalition and, if possible, under the aegis of the UN or at least a regional organisation. So, the decision to intervene is rarely taken alone. Within a coalition, there will need to be an agreed definition of the problem and the optimum solutions as well as a set of complementary and adequate capabilities. A 'coalition of the willing', to use the current terminology, may be a good start, but it should also be a coalition of the ready and able. Putting such

*searching for a coalition of the willing, ready and able*

coalitions together takes time, and may lead to an over-dramatisation of the threat as well as intensive arm-twisting. As soon as an objective has been set, the reputation of the coalition members and the sponsoring institution, if there is one, is at stake. Even with the most modest ventures, the consequences of failure can be long-term and damaging, especially if another coalition is required to meet another crisis.

Most interventions require the consent of the most substantial regional actors. *Desert Storm* depended on the active support of Saudi Arabia and other regional states, and this was one factor in the promise to confine operations to the expulsion of Iraqi forces from Kuwait, rather than the liberation of Iraq from Saddam's regime. When action was being considered by the US in the face of North Korea's evident breaches of the provisions of the Nuclear Non-Proliferation Treaty (NPT) in the early 1990s, its options were limited by the evident reluctance of regional powers, including

South Korea but also China and Japan, to countenance the use of force.

Although 'high-intensity' operations are often linked with rule enforcement and 'low-intensity' operations with maintaining civil order against groups that have adopted guerrilla or terrorist tactics, this is a false dichotomy. Forces designed for high-intensity war can be suitable for a range of conflicts, in so far as mobility, protection and concentrated firepower are required. *Stinger* missiles being transported by Afghan *mujahidin* on mules, or Somalia's General Mohammed Farrah Aideed communicating with his followers using a 'combination of couriers, low-power cellular phones and drums', provide eloquent images of high and low technology working together.[6] The more portable the weapons, the more widely they will be spread.

The real distinction may be between those wars conducted apart from civil society, and those conducted within it. In the case of the former, a victory on the battlefield may be decisive; in the latter case, the outcome may depend on the comparative ability of societies to withstand the stresses and strains of war, including direct attacks.

## Asymmetric Strategies

Thus, asymmetries of power and interest in a conflict can come together in asymmetries of strategy. The result is an 'asymmetric war'. This concept has become something of a cliché by force of circumstances. As other countries cannot fight on US terms, if they have to fight US forces, they must do so differently. It is also extremely difficult to envisage a truly symmetrical war, which would be over an agreed object of equal value to two sides of equal capability, as if war could be a team game in which two sides are allowed equal numbers of players and play on a level field according to agreed rules enforced by an independent referee. In international conflict, two sides with equivalent capabilities and interests are difficult enough to imagine, let alone agreed rules and an impartial referee.

In the official US version, symmetrical engagements are between similar types of forces, so that superior numbers, training, leadership and technology will largely determine the outcome. Asymmetrical engagements are between dissimilar forces. Here, the outcome is the result of an inability to defend against the force with

The Revolution in Strategic Affairs **39**

which attacked.[7] This focuses on means rather than on ends, and as such is apolitical. In an asymmetric war, the differences may lie in means rather than in ends, for example in a dispute over a piece of land, but two sides might prepare to wage war in the same way with quite different views about what is at stake. The same conflict may be about regime survival for one belligerent, territorial gain for another and international order for an intervening power. As likely, there will be disparities in both means and ends.

*can wars be fought according to Western preferences?*

The association of symmetry with stability is the consequence of four decades of mutual nuclear deterrence, when the search for a decisive asymmetry came to nought and was anyway judged to be too dangerous. Even with a symmetry of interests, however, a symmetry of conventional capabilities tends to become unstable over time for, if sustained, the result would be stalemate and the prospect of mutual attrition. Victory depends on creating an asymmetry that works to one's advantage. Even though the same moves might be available to both sides – mobilising extra resources, courting allies, trying innovative tactics – their implications and potential advantages will vary. Even when there is pressure to converge on a particular set of capabilities or type of battle, this will rarely have equivalent meaning for the two sides.

At the start of the 1960s, for example, the US became convinced that Soviet efforts were coming to be concentrated in insurgencies in the Third World. This led to investment in counter-insurgency capabilities, so as to be able to fight the insurgents on their own terms, and so to intense interest in the conduct of guerrilla warfare Yet when the US found itself in Vietnam, facing a substantial insurgency directed against one of its most important Third World clients, neither its immediate objectives nor its apparent comparative advantage led to an effective counter-insurgency. When the communists were tempted into open battle with US forces they often suffered badly, but when they kept to guerrilla methods and prepared for the long haul, the Americans were left vexed and frustrated. Because there seemed to be no end to the conflict, casualties were being taken without the compensation of a decisive victory. In the end, South Vietnam mattered far more to North

Vietnam than it did to the US. The key asymmetry was in the stakes of the belligerents in the outcome of the conflict.[8]

When facing Western states with overwhelming strength but underwhelming commitment, it will always make sense to avoid open battle and to concentrate instead on raising the costs to the point where Western losses outweigh potential gains. Saddam explored strategies in 1990–91 designed to undermine the political cohesion of the coalition and the will of its individual members: encouraging wishful thinking on the scope for a diplomatic compromise; promising 'the mother of all battles'; and threatening a campaign of terror against the coalition's home populations, the use of weapons of mass destruction (WMD) and severe environmental damage.

These failed because Iraq lacked the political and military capacity to implement them effectively. Even so, generating fear in the West of the dire fate awaiting troops sent into Iraqi 'killing zones' almost had a successful deterrent effect. Scrappy ballistic-missile attacks caused a massive diversion of Western military effort and substantial preparations had to be made to counter attempts to use chemical or bacteriological weapons. Anxiety over terror tactics kept the bulk of the US population effectively grounded because of fears of flying on vulnerable commercial airlines, while releasing oil into the Gulf and setting wells on fire underlined the threat that Iraq posed to the Gulf's ecology.

During the mid-1990s, the Bosnian Serbs identified the factors inhibiting a full-blooded Western response to their campaign of 'ethnic cleansing'. They played on memories of the German Army being held down by Tito's partisans during the Second World War to threaten a 'quagmire'. To ward off air attacks, they offered timely diplomatic concessions, while holding Bosnian cities and UN peacekeepers (who were unable to defend themselves) hostage to Western restraint. They followed the Iraqis by locating some of their most important assets close to highly populated areas. Eventually, an intensive air campaign helped to convince the Serbs to agree to the Dayton talks in 1995. In one sense, this campaign drew on RMA-type developments. Critical reconnaissance was carried out using unmanned aerial vehicles (UAVs), while precision munitions kept down casualties. In another sense, the result reflected more basic factors, notably the Croatian Army's advance and the reorganisation of Western ground forces on UN duty into a serious fighting force.

These alternative strategies reflect those that the weak have consistently adopted against the strong: concentrating on imposing pain rather than winning battles; gaining time rather than moving to closure; targeting the enemy's domestic political base as much as his forward military capabilities; relying on his intolerance of casualties and his weaker stake in the resolution of the conflict; and playing

*the strategy of the weak against the strong*

on a reluctance to cause civilian suffering, even if it restricts military options. In short, whereas stronger military powers have a natural preference for decisive battlefield victories, the weaker are more ready to draw the civilian sphere into the conflict, while avoiding open battle.

## Options for the Weak

If the problem for the West is not the ability to prevail as such, but to do so at a tolerable cost, opponents may need to do little more than keep going, avoiding a definitive defeat while continuing to cause pain. Ralph Peters argues that Western forces must prepare to face 'warriors', whom he characterises colourfully as 'erratic primitives of shifting allegiances, habituated to violence, with no stake in civil order'. Peters describes their approach to war in terms familiar to students of guerrilla warfare. They only stand and fight when they have an overwhelming advantage:

> *Instead they snipe, ambush, mislead, and betray, attempting to fool the constrained soldiers confronting them into alienating the local population or allies, while otherwise hunkering down and trying to outlast the organized military forces pitted against them.*[9]

This overstates the problem. Some may enjoy fighting for its own sake, but the most fearsome warriors are likely to be fighting for a cause or a way of life they hold dear. The performance of guerrilla bands, militias and popular armies is actually quite mixed. The experience of counter-insurgency warfare, especially with regard to Vietnam, may not be hopeful in terms of persuading a military establishment to adopt unfamiliar operational forms in order to cope with an enemy unwilling to fight in open battle, but it also tends to confirm that irregular warfare requires popular support as a source of recruits, supplies and places to hide.[10]

Earl Tilford observes that, since the Second World War, 'US military failures have come at the hands of opponents who had little or no air or sea forces and whose ground forces were composed largely of light infantry'.[11] Stephen Biddle argues that Iraqi forces might have fared much better if they had been better trained. US technological advantages, he argues, were important largely in magnifying the effects of Iraqi errors. More sensible defensive preparations and greater skill in combat would have enabled the Iraqis to inflict substantial casualties, even if they had not actually won.[12]

Elsewhere, Biddle has challenged the presumption that only educationally advanced states can cope with advanced technology, referring to Afghanistan and Vietnam, where local fighters made innovative use of modern systems. Much depends on the quality of civil–military relations. A cohesive society can produce determined fighters, while an insecure dictatorship squanders its military strength as the political leadership becomes fearful of the officer corps and seeks to keep it divided and isolated, with promotion on the basis of loyalty rather than competence.[13]

One of the reasons why the liberation of Kuwait in 1991 was not followed by the liberation of Iraq was a fear that the Iraqi forces would have been more highly motivated and better positioned in defence of their homeland. Whether this would have been true in this case, in general an intimate knowledge of terrain has always been considered an advantage in combat. In addition, certain types of terrain do not favour Western strengths. Peters warns that one of the critical features of the modern world is urbanisation, yet the US armed forces long for 'gallant struggles in green fields' rather than grim cityscapes.[14] Urban combat remains manpower-intensive. It requires 'great multiples of small durables and disposables' rather than large numbers of 'glamorous big-ticket systems'. The US National Defense Panel puts great stress on the hazards of urban environments:

*The maze of streets, crush of population, and complex of buildings and vertical and subterranean constructions present a demanding landscape that has the capacity to absorb ground forces, confound the effectiveness of stand-off weapons, and slow operations to a virtual standstill.*[15]

Cities complicate targeting and manoeuvring. They are full of 'noncombatants, vital infrastructures, and government and nongovernment institutions', all of which might hamper the employment of force along Western lines.[16] So concerned is the Panel that it sees diverting war into an urban setting as a natural part of an opponent's asymmetric strategy and something it believes that US forces might best leave to local allies. Allies might be relieved to note that the US Marines have started to focus on urban warfare as the latest stage in the *Sea Dragon* programme to develop new forms of expeditionary warfare.[17]

The setting for military operations will determine the advantage provided through access to the new technology. Known, fixed targets and large expensive platforms that remain exposed while they move will be vulnerable to stand-off systems, but less so small and passive systems that do not draw attention to themselves and can merge into the background. As Martin Libicki observes, on this basis, 'infiltration across sea will become more difficult than infiltration across land and jungles, forests and cities more problematic than deserts'.[18] As, traditionally, invading forces have required substantial concentrations of heavy forces, this puts a query against such excursions in the future because they will be so blatant as to be 'eaten whole by a US military with dominant battlespace knowledge'.

On the other hand, Libicki notes, 'light forces that can evade US systems' will be 'insufficient to outgun forces on the other side'. From this he argues that: 'The more that our ability to see forces a difficult choice between these two force structures, the better the chance for regional stability'.[19] Rule enforcement should therefore be reinforced, if aggression across borders becomes easier to deter, and if necessary thwart, because of the transparency and thus vulnerability of offensive forces.

This is an updated version of an argument, popular since the 1970s, to which there have always been two substantial objections.

The first draws on another familiar debate, that over whether new technology favours the defence. The analytical question appears straightforward when phrased in terms of defending a piece of territory against an invader, but becomes less so as soon as it is recognised that a defender might also have to move forces in order to pre-empt an imminent attack, cut off an invader, liberate territory that has already been captured or come to the aid of an ally. Although the attempt is often made, labelling types of equipment or partial capabilities as being truly defensive or offensive tends to be misleading.[20]

The second problem is that the US can notice a force being prepared to move against a neighbour, but still fail to act. There was no shortage of indicators that Iraq was in a position to attack Kuwait. The reason that so little was done to warn Iraq off was not a lack of information but a complacent assessment and a hesitant policy. The result was a need to react to a *fait accompli*, which meant that dislodging Iraq from Kuwait would involve taking the offensive. Domestic opinion and also allies required some persuading that this was at all a wise thing to do. So whatever the possibilities for 'real-time' military decision and action, policy formulation and political persuasion tend to take time. The demands of coalition-formation mean that the initiative may be difficult to seize from a local aggressor.

Force still has to be despatched. Speed of mobilisation was always recognised to be NATO's basic difficulty in responding in a timely fashion to indicators of imminent Warsaw Pact aggression, leading in the 1970s to fears of being caught by a 'standing start' attack. Not only is 'real-time logistics' impossible, but the advances in the movement of personnel and *matériel* into battle have not been anything like as substantial as those in mounting operations on arrival. This encourages reliance on the much-extended ranges of missiles and aircraft from home bases, or on naval task forces, one factor arguing for the retention of long-range aircraft and carrier groups. Stand-off weapons can rarely substitute for troops on the ground, however, and once this requirement is set there is always a risk of the situation deteriorating during the period from embarkation to disembarkation. Moving personnel and equipment into a battlespace is hazardous against a prepared local opponent, especially if a delayed reaction allows the enemy to gear himself to disrupting their entry, including possibly mined waters and alert air defences.[21]

The apparent Western advantages in conventional military strength must therefore be qualified by reference to the opportunities available to a determined and intelligent opponent to take advantage of local conditions and to use the advance notice that an expeditionary force is on its way to prepare an unpleasant welcome.

## The Threat of Mass Destruction

To the arguments against Western countries becoming involved in distant conflicts – the hostile reception forces will face and the risk of being bogged down in an inconclusive and murky form of combat – is normally added the prospect of retaliation with WMD. An Indian General is reported to have observed that the lesson of the Gulf War was 'Never fight the US without nuclear weapons'.[22]

Yet the war left Washington focusing on non-nuclear possibilities: the Western Way of Warfare implies the progressive marginalisation – and elimination – of nuclear weapons as a factor in international politics. Fred Iklé has expressed concern that the RMA literature contains 'scarcely a thought about nuclear or other mass destruction weapons, save for a shy aside'. Just because nuclear weapons were encapsulated within a 'cocoon of non-use' and deterrence worked against the Soviet Union, there is no guarantee that it will be successful against new enemies in new political circumstances.[23] For a country fearing that it risks being on the receiving end of US military power, the deterrent effect of a nuclear capacity retains a certain attraction, just as it attracted the US when it deemed itself to be conventionally inferior to the Warsaw Pact. Severe Russian inferiority in conventional capabilities has now stimulated a greater readiness in Moscow to rely on its nuclear arsenal as the ultimate source of security.[24]

The possibility of a 'seepage' of nuclear technology and expertise from the former Soviet Union and revelations about the Iraqi and North Korean nuclear programmes have kept the dangers of nuclear proliferation at the forefront of Western security thinking. Yet this has started to be matched by a sense that biological weapons offer an easier route to a mass-destruction capability. This concern was underlined between November 1997 and February 1998 as the US and UK stepped up the pressure on Iraq to comply with UN weapons inspectors then searching for biological weapons. It became apparent that, compared with a nuclear programme, a biological-weapons programme was much easier to conceal because it involved portable facilities and products.

This concern grows when attention shifts from rogue states to terrorist groups. How porous the arms-control regimes will be when it comes to dealing with nuclear, chemical and biological weapons remains to be seen, especially when they must take into account non-state actors as well as states. Non-state actors are unlikely to obtain nuclear weapons, given the technical and financial requirements of doing so, but may find chemical or biological weapons more accessible. 'This may not be the stuff of the heroic gesture beloved by past terrorist groups', observes Walter Laquer, 'but what of groups whose motivation is less political and who follow aberrant philosophies?'[25]

Richard Betts believes the biological-weapons threat to be so serious that it could create a US vulnerability that 'might require pulling back from involvement in some foreign conflicts'. Betts cites a 1993 study that concluded that one aircraft delivering 100 kilograms of anthrax spores over Washington DC could kill up to three million people.[26] There are other potential nightmares that fall short of mass destruction, involving criminal organisations and religious extremists, followers of cults and the psychologically disturbed, disaffected ethnic groups and regional secessionists. They might have rationales and opportunities for disruptive and violent activities that can cause pain and panic, and may take in countries only tangentially related to their conflicts.

The US no longer has chemical and biological weapons, but it does possess a formidable nuclear arsenal. This is seen to deter direct nuclear threats against the US, and also to provide some form of nuclear guarantee to allies and clients.[27] Does it have a role in deterring chemical and biological-weapons use? The most recent Presidential guidelines for the targeting of US nuclear weapons, issued in November 1997, are said to contain language 'that would permit US nuclear strikes after enemy attacks using chemical or biological weapons'.[28] Furthermore, Iraq has claimed that it was deterred from using chemical weapons during the Gulf War because of fear of US (and possibly Israeli) nuclear retaliation. William Arkin suggests that the idea that such attacks could only be deterred with nuclear threats appealed to the Iraqi regime's egotism.[29] It would be surprising if there had not been an element of real deterrence at work here. The difficulty lies in weighing it against other factors, including technical and operational difficulties and the Bush administration's warning to Saddam that any WMD use would provide justification for a formal extension of the war aims to include the toppling of the regime.

It is hard to see how Western countries can make explicit nuclear threats to deter chemical or biological weapons use. Apart from legal obligations not to use nuclear weapons against non-nuclear states, it would be difficult to make retaliation automatic, given that such an attack might turn out to be poorly targeted and to have limited results. Nonetheless, at the same time it would be unwise for any would-be perpetrator to assume that an attack which caused immense suffering and a vast loss of life would not generate such anger that nuclear use would become a real possibility. In practice, Western governments are likely to rely largely on active non-proliferation measures, the development of a range of conventional military responses and protective measures to limit the potential damage to their troops in the field and to their wider societies.

The logic of these developments was thrown into relief in February 1998, when US and British forces prepared strikes against Iraq to coerce it into removing restrictions on UN weapons inspections. Iraq had no serious means of resisting allied strikes. The allies, however, lacked the 'dominant situational awareness' that would have allowed them to identify all likely sites of chemical and biological weapons and attack them with confidence. They were therefore forced to rely on threats of punitive raids that risked being denounced as excessive at home as well as in the wider international community. At the same time, lack of confidence that the offending Iraqi capabilities would be removed by military means prompted Israel and Kuwait to rush to take protective measures. The threats, when combined with some diplomatic inducements, worked, but the strategic position for the allies was uncomfortable.

The Western Way of Warfare, with its desire to confine warfare to professional combatants, points to decisive battlefield victories. Not only do the circumstances of contemporary conflict imply much more interaction with civil society, and a greater difficulty in separating combatants from non-combatants, but also so does past experience of war. Whatever the intentions of belligerents, it can be difficult to prevent a conflict spilling over into civil society. Attacks on power supplies, communication nodes and the transport system can all be justified by the need to disable enemy armed forces. Few advancing armies have the time or the inclination to skirt around civilian obstacles in their path. Most seriously, when a country is in desperate straits and facing defeat in conventional war, attacking the enemy's society can appear to be the only remaining option. All these reasons help explain why the history of war in the twentieth century is so discouraging to those who believe that armed force can be used decisively, while being contained in its effects.

## chapter 4

# Information Warfare

Information warfare is now presented as a distinct form of conflict. This was given formal status by the Pentagon in 1992, and there is now a US Army Field Manual (FM 100-6) devoted to Information Operations.[1] These are defined as

> *continuous military operations within the MIE [Military Information Environment] that enable, enhance, and protect the friendly force's ability to collect, process and act on information to achieve an advantage across the range of military operations. IO include[s] interacting with the global information environment and exploiting or denying an adversary's information and decision capabilities.*[2]

The MIE will offer remarkable capabilities to quite junior commanders. They will be able to 'push' information out of the military equivalent of direct-satellite television, with channels for meteorology and updates on air defences, and 'pull' information from a variety of data-sets to produce a view of the most relevant parts of their battlespace. But this will be but one part of a Global Information Environment – 'a world-wide network of information sources, archives, consumers and architectures'.[3] Here is to be found unprecedented inter-connectivity which leaps across national and institutional borders and blurs distinctions between the civilian and military sectors.

This chapter examines two propositions. The first is that the information revolution is reinforcing the best aspects of the Western Way of Warfare, encouraging tendencies towards efficiency, discriminating use of weapons and low casualties. The second is that, at the same time, it is opening up new types of vulnerabilities which an opponent will be tempted to exploit.

There is a danger in exaggerating both the novelty of the information revolution in military affairs, and in particular the difference that information can make on its own. By itself, it does not energise, destroy, shelter or move forces, though it can provide vital support to all these functions. Commanders have always sought to protect their capacity to collect, transmit and apply vital information and attack that of the enemy. The current debate on information warfare tends to follow well-established areas of interest, such as command and control, intelligence and psychological warfare, or else suggests activities with rather vague purposes.[4]

It also follows the tendency of those debates over most innovations, marked particularly with first aircraft and then nuclear weapons, as to whether their main role would be largely 'tactical', in support of general-purpose forces, or 'strategic', winning wars by themselves through direct attacks on the enemy's most sensitive points. Thus, some commentators consider information war as a support to overall military operations, while others consider 'strategic information operations' to be potentially decisive by themselves.[5]

## From Deficit to Surplus

Information is becoming less of a privileged resource as more people have more means of tapping into more forms. Military-relevant information can be obtained through the civilian sphere and shared by friend and foe. The immediate dissemination of data of a high intelligence value on the Cable News Network (CNN) and other news channels has come to be taken for granted. The number of commercial receivers for the *NAVSTAR* GPS now far exceeds that of military receivers and, while their accuracy is not as great, it is still good.

Attempts to limit access to these services are undermined by the intensity of commercial imperatives, which include demands for contractual guarantees, and also the development of competition. Relatively sophisticated forms of encryption have become available commercially in order to safeguard financially sensitive communications. They could also safeguard other types of communication.

With satellite imagery, the demand for an uninterrupted service, unimpeded by considerations of national policy, has limited efforts at restrictions. If US satellite images come with too many restrictions, it is possible to turn to services from France, India and Russia. Commercial launches exceeded government launches of satellites in 1996 for the first time in history. At the end of 1997, the world's first civilian spy satellite was launched by Colorado company EarthWatch Incorporated atop a Russian rocket. It is claimed to offer military-quality resolution. In peacetime, there appear to be few restrictions on the images that can be acquired and marketed. The US government has retained the right to screen foreign customers, although it is not difficult to imagine how any export prohibitions could be circumvented. In times of war, the government can order the cameras to be switched off. At least six such satellites could be operating within a few years.[6]

A September 1997 wargame organised by the US Army featured an enemy with no organic military space capability, but able to use commercially available communication and navigation satellites. This highlighted the problems of denying access to one and not to everyone else: the enemy was able to develop an impressive communications network using cellular telephones, which could not be singled out for jamming.[7]

Satellite imagery still poses special problems of collection and interpretation, but GPS will go the way of radios, mobile telephones and personal computers and become portable and widely available.[8] There are now some 150 million computers worldwide, where 25 years ago there were barely 50,000. The power of some of the smallest of these is equivalent to types that not long ago were subject to the most stringent export-licensing controls. As many as 70m people use the Internet, already a tenth of the number using telephones.[9]

The quality of civilian information systems tends to be so good that even military organisations use them. Commanders find that information from the British Broadcasting Corporation (BBC) arrives quicker than that passing through the military hierarchy and arriving in filtered form. The Pentagon relies on commercial telecommunications for 95% of its information traffic.[10]

The degree to which finance, trade, transport and energy supply rely upon the smooth functioning of information technology can be seen whenever a critical system crashes, or in the anticipation of the 'millennium bug'. In strategic thinking, dependence soon becomes a vulnerability and, by extension, a potential target. In the 1970s, action by the Organisation of Petroleum Exporting Countries (OPEC) suddenly made Western states aware of their dependence on external oil supplies. 'Energy security' became a major concern until new sources of supply and conservation measures eased the threat. Now, without any severe warning shots, the same translation from dependence to target has been made with information. Some of the more excitable analysts, noting the importance of complex information systems to all aspects of modern society, have imagined the consequences of their sudden absence, and concluded from this that they have identified a natural target for an inventive and resourceful belligerent.

## Interfering with Information
### Anti-Satellite Systems

Satellites are unarmed and easily tracked, yet essential for navigation, intelligence, meteorology and communications. As soon as this military infrastructure began to be placed in space, it was assumed by many that military logic pointed to a concerted effort to bring it down. Both superpowers developed rather primitive anti-satellite systems; the US continues to explore more advanced types.

Yet these systems are unlikely to be employable on such a scale that they become much more than nuisances. Destroying a satellite in space would be an unambiguously hostile act, and would therefore escalate a crisis. Unless the anti-satellite systems had been thoroughly tested beforehand, it would be surprising if an opponent would dare to rely on them. There would need to be confidence that the enemy would be left effectively blind, deaf and dumb after the attack, so there would be no margin for error.

The conviction that, in the future, the US will 'fight in space, from space, and into space' still has its adherents, but there is no reason to suppose that it is any more credible now than it was when first proclaimed 40 years ago.[11] Ideas about great battles being fought in the heavens, deciding the fate of nations and the course of history (perhaps without damage to life on Earth), developed with the space age, and have been regularly revived. In June 1975, the Pentagon's Malcolm Currie commented: 'over the next ten or fifteen years space is not going to remain the unmolested territory, the sanctuary, that it is today'.[12] Twenty years later, in *New World Vistas*, a USAF project, can be found the claim that the 'domain of conflict is now moving from earth into space and now into cyberspace' and a vision of a 'Future Force' that will:

> *eventually contain space, ground, and airborne weapons that can project photon energy, kinetic energy, and information against space and ground assets. Many space and information weapons will destroy. Others will confuse the enemy and weave the 'bodyguard of lies' that will protect our forces.*

The text of this document gives little support to any early prospect of space weapons. If directing kinetic-energy weapons to Earth, the obvious base is also Earth, using current methods such as an intercontinental ballistic missile (ICBM), which has half the response time of orbital weapons and far lower readiness costs.

*New World Vistas* claims that directed-energy weapons offer 'attractive features such as reusability, speed-of-light response, and training and testing features'. However, as became apparent during the great SDI debate, deploying lasers plus optics and control systems in space 'will involve significant problems in logistics, resupply, and training in addition to those of targeting and control'. The cost would be high and the energy-storage problems formidable.

An alternative course would be to construct the laser system on the ground and then deploy targeting mirrors in space. This would be logistically more straightforward, as the most complex elements would be on the ground, and would increase the choice of type of laser. So, if directed energy is beamed to Earth from space, it will have first been sent to space from the ground and relayed back by means of mirrors. Naturally enough, *New World Vistas* stops short of actually advocating such a system, let alone attempting to construct the arguments that would persuade Congress to fund it.

Kinetic and directed energy are also the two means of attacking satellites directly: kinetic energy has been used in past anti-satellite systems that place projectiles or fragments into the path of the hostile satellite. They are expensive: the attack vehicles are complex, the process depends on high-quality tracking and guidance and, particularly important, readiness must be maintained to launch as quickly as possible. Directed-energy systems require considerable power (a megawatt or more) and precision tracking and pointing systems that have yet to be developed. Ground-based directed-energy weapons can be developed, and *New World Vistas* recommends that this be done, though with little discussion of counter-measures, such as stealth techniques, or how they could be employed.

The document notes that few countries are likely to develop anti-satellite systems. Indeed, it is difficult to imagine any country other than Russia even considering such an enterprise. The Soviet system that was developed only threatened satellites in orbits below 5,000km, which would include some photo-reconnaissance, meteorology, geodesy and electronic-intelligence satellites as well as manned spacecraft. It is much harder to see how satellites in semi-synchronous orbits (about 20,000km altitude), for example *NAVSTAR*, or geosynchronous orbits (36,000km), where communications and early-warning systems are to be found, could be put seriously at risk.[13]

Information being transmitted from or through satellite systems may be attacked at the point of its reception on the ground. Opponents might attempt to interfere using tailored electronic means. A more crude destructive means would be the use of the electromagnetic pulse (EMP) from a nuclear detonation to disrupt all communications, though the means required to achieve this would hardly be dismissed as merely an act of information warfare. Generating an EMP by non-nuclear means such as High Energy Radio Frequency (HERF) 'guns' lacks the output of nuclear methods.

## Strategic Information Warfare

John Deutch, as Director of Central Intelligence, offered his view that the electron is the 'ultimate precision-guided weapon'. It can be aimed directly 'at the command and brain structure of our military systems and our military forces'.[14] The sophistication and ingenuity of hackers and the inventors of viruses are notoriously impressive. Hackers can explore the weak points of any complex system, hoping that one combination of identification and password will provide a route into a forbidden area. Viruses now appear as 'Trojan Horses', hidden within a host programme and triggered upon execution; 'worms', which obliterate or alter data as they bore through system memory; and 'logic bombs', which embed themselves in an executable file until activated by a specific event, such as a date. Most viruses are 'dumb' rather than 'smart'. They in effect destroy on impact, but eventually could become smarter, responding to their environment within a computer.[15]

Small information-warfare campaigns are quite common-place: the mischievous hacker trying to alter examination marks or bank accounts; the manic inventor of viruses; or the extortionist demanding large sums of money from companies by threatening to cripple vital software. Microsoft has been targeted – in part to demonstrate the danger of relying on a hegemonic supplier, whose standard systems are well understood and share known vulnerabilities. Tobacco companies suffer regular electronic attacks. The Pentagon's communication systems appear to be under almost continual bombardment from hackers, who see them as a special challenge. The bulk of these attacks are unsuccessful, although occasionally one gets through the outer barriers. Other parts of the government machine may have more trouble. The Environmental Protection Agency suddenly found its website shut down in 1996.[16]

It is not hard to imagine the same techniques being adopted for overt political purposes by sub-state groups, and these techniques might even be applied in a regular war.[17] Disabling air-defence systems, sending missiles off-course, leaving local commanders in the dark and senior commanders confused by interfering with software or causing catastrophic hardware malfunctions have obvious appeal. The fear of being the victim of such an attack is also a powerful motivating force. A Chinese journal has referred to how a 'digitised force' might be attacked once a set of communications equipment has been obtained, after which enemy information can be stolen or falsified.[18]

Outside of the military sphere, strategic information war might seek to cause a collapse of the banking system or the loss of air-traffic control or power transmission. Other ideas are more manipulative, interfering with the content of information processes rather than their form. 'Semantic attacks' allow an external agent to control a system that appears to insiders to be working normally.

*'semantic attacks' and 'neocortical warfare'*

Television images might be distorted to make an enemy leader appear ridiculous; misleading signals could be sent to top executives or even Generals; false orders might be delivered to key units; black propaganda might be spread about one section of society to another. One author has sought to advance claims for 'neocortical warfare' that 'strives to *control* or *shape* the behavior of enemy organisms, but without destroying the organisms'. The focus would be on enemy minds rather than capabilities.[19] This is derivative of psychological warfare.

In all these cases, it is possible to imagine the relevant capabilities playing some sort of supportive role in certain conflicts, but extremely difficult to imagine them carrying the whole burden of protecting a nation's security by themselves.[20] Information systems do not always represent easy targets, especially as users learn to take more precautions – by reducing their dependence upon single systems, continually backing up electronic information, and keeping open a number of lines of communication and sources of information. Most large organisations accept that they must take measures to control access and prevent misuse, to detect and eliminate viruses, and generally to prevent any malfunctions, whether or not premeditated and engineered, from having catastrophic consequences.

There is an unavoidable degree of uncertainty surrounding any attempt to interfere with another's information networks. Have the right systems been targeted? How dependent is the enemy upon them? Might interference become apparent before the critical moment and any damage rectified? Is it possible to become the victim of a double bluff?

For these reasons, there will be a reluctance to rely solely on information-warfare operations, no matter how brilliant in conception. For perception-manipulation to work, it is necessary to have a good understanding of the cognitive framework of the target, otherwise bogus messages will soon become obvious. With much information being so widely shared, deliberate errors could also soon become widely shared, and even 'blow back' to confuse the sender. The more information-warfare measures are adopted, the more governments and other organisations will become sensitive to the risk that information has been deliberately compromised (a familiar problem with espionage). This could reach the point where the integrity of the most innocent information is doubted. It would be paradoxical if the rapid improvements in the accessibility and quality of information were negated because so little of it could be trusted.[21]

Even if a successful strategic information campaign could be designed and mounted, there could be no guarantee that a victim would respond in kind, rather than with whatever means happened to be available. It cannot be assumed that the response to these, as with other 'non-lethal' weapons, will be of equivalent 'non-lethality'. Furthermore, when faced with the task of disabling a critical facility, clever and subtle forms of electronic warfare may well seem unnecessarily risky when compared with something cruder, simpler and probably more violent. Why be a hacker when you can use a bomb? Traditional techniques of concealment and deception may prove to be simpler means of confusing an opponent.

The countries most at risk from information attacks may not be the advanced Western states, but those increasingly dependent upon information technology yet still behind in indigenous capabilities. Not surprisingly, given past sensitivities to this issue, Russian Generals are particularly concerned about the vulnerability of their country to this type of attack, and so warn of the risk of a 'strategic' response of a different sort. Timothy Thomas cites a Russian theoretician warning of

> the possible catastrophic consequences of the uses of strategic information warfare means by an enemy, whether on economic or state command and control systems, or on the combat potential of the armed forces ... Russia retains the right to use nuclear weapons first against the means and forces of information warfare, and then against the aggressor state itself.[22]

An example of a failure to grasp the danger of insecure communications came when the Russians attacked the aircraft of

Dzhokar Dudayev, the Chechen rebel leader, because he had revealed his position by using his mobile telephone.

Given the steady erosion of the barriers between civilian and military networks, it can be assumed that offensive and defensive operations will share much in common whether campaigns are being waged against rival corporations, international criminal gangs or rogue states. The integration of civilian and military information networks is, in itself, a development of major significance. The growing use of Commercial Off The Shelf (COTS) technology solutions by the military adds to the risks of importing viruses, and also that familiar systems with known vulnerabilities will be in use. There will be a case (which may also include the need for hardening against EMP effects) for keeping the most sensitive information flows and key command and control relationships on separate networks. The pressures for cost-savings, however, are likely to reduce steadily the amount of dedicated military hardware.

The best advice for the military may be to learn to live with the consequences of the increasing openness of information, rather than hoping for the capacity to bring about its sudden denial. Officers are already learning to adjust to the all-pervading character of the modern media. One day, they may successfully demonstrate their determination to ensure pin-point accuracy by showing videotapes of 'smart' attacks on command centres; the next, they may be responding to television footage of the human cost of another missile taking a wrong turning. The same television stations carry the claims of all sides in a conflict and, as a matter of course, show military operations from the perspective both of those launching them and of those on the receiving end. Operational secrecy now requires the active connivance of the media.

The National Defense Panel asserts that responding to 'information warfare threats to the United States may present the greatest challenge in preparing for the security environment of 2010-2020'. Yet it adds that the 'threat is diffuse and difficult to identify'. Its discussion of this point, and related topics such as 'space control', suggests that current thinking has not gone much beyond asserting desiderata – we must deny to our enemies what we must protect for ourselves – without a clear analysis of what is really at stake or what is militarily practicable in areas moving out of the control of all governments. The most profound strategic effects of the information revolution have occurred not so much because of a deliberate campaign or the implementation of a master-plan, but as a natural consequence of the intense inter-penetration of societies, encouraged not only by the nature of the global economy but also by the ease of access to the Internet and the information that it contains. The flows of information in, around and between belligerents are unlikely to be controllable. This works more to the detriment of the closed, than of the open, society.

In short, the multiplication of channels through which information can pass not only reduces dependence upon a single channel, but also the opportunities to control the flow. Unlike commodities such as fuel, food, spare parts and ammunition, which are finite resources normally in deficit and which can only be moved to where they are most needed by specific forms of transport, information is much easier to generate, transmit and collect. The problems are more likely to do with superfluity than with deficiency. There are few information 'choke points', no easily obtained 'command of info-power', no 'centre of gravity' to be targeted.

Speculative works on the future conduct of warfare that ask only 'how' and 'with what' questions, and fail to consider the 'who', 'whom' and 'why', soon lose touch with reality. At the start of the 1980s, in the context of the debates on space warfare, Michael May observed the problems caused by the

> *interjection of sensational, out-of-context events, often technical, sometimes non-technical: the two high-altitude nuclear bursts that wipe out all communications, the space mines that suddenly explode, the saboteur who destroys the key node. These 'sensations' have foundations in fact. But if we are to maintain any hope of spending our money sensibly we must ask, when considering them: under what circumstances could they occur? What else would be happening then? How lasting and how widespread would their effects be?*[23]

More recently, much writing on information warfare has been criticised for being 'beyond plausibility'. Measures are proposed that might paralyse or confuse an adversary, but with little thought given to 'entirely unanticipated results or even to consequences that would be inconsistent with or counterproductive to the original intent'.[24]

## Information and Friction

The ancient Chinese strategist Sun Tzu, much beloved of modern 'cyber-warriors' as well as management theorists, offered many observations on how to acquire and use information (or more usefully 'knowledge'), including concealment, confusion, deception, dissimulation and generally staying inscrutable.[25] He can be taken too seriously. Consider, for example, statements such as 'Know the enemy and know yourself; in a hundred battles you will never be in peril', which appeared at the top of a section on information warfare in a recent publication of the US Joint Chiefs of Staff.

Sun Tzu believed that perfect knowledge could be obtained. This could then be used to calculate the likely outcome of a battle through a process that would now be described as net assessment. In spite of the information revolution, perfect knowledge remains an impossibility (because information must always be selected and ordered through imperfect conceptual frameworks), while the results of battles are rarely wholly predictable and, even when they are, they cannot always be avoided.[26]

Nineteenth-century Prussian military theorist Carl von Clausewitz did not believe that the outcome of war could be calculable. At the heart of his analysis was a keen sense of war's unpredictability, and the role of *the importance of chance, guesswork and luck* chance, guesswork and luck. This was bound up with his concept of 'friction', the most persistent and perplexing feature of war – 'all the factors that distinguish real war from war on paper'. The unreliability of information contributed to friction:

> *Many intelligence reports in war are contradictory; even more are false, and most are uncertain. This is true of all intelligence but even more so in the heat of battle, where such reports tend to contradict and cancel each other out. In short, most intelligence is false, and the effect of fear is to multiply lies and inaccuracies.*[27]

Does the information age represent the triumph of Sun Tzu over Clausewitz? The RMA promises ever more timely and pertinent information at all levels, and the ability to communicate directly, constantly and instantaneously through the chain of command. Enthusiasts hover on the edge of pronouncing the 'fog of war' lifted and the problem of 'friction' solved. This is unlikely. The possibilities for misunderstanding and mistakes remain, and the growing dependence upon the management of information means that the impact of any errors may well be magnified.

There are new sources of friction. The sort of information that previous commanders might have dreamt about receiving in good time will be available almost immediately. But there can be too much of the wrong sort and too little of the right sort, which somehow must be retrieved and then comprehended from all that is received. This is the familiar intelligence problem of 'noise' magnified many times. It can lead to information dependence, whereby it is assumed that the next piece will provide the final clue and make a difficult decision easier. Intuition and hunch become more suspect, for there appears to be less excuse for ignorance. Yet in high-tempo war, there will be reluctance to wait for even more information and few opportunities for considered reflection of the information received, or to address the ambiguity that it will inevitably contain. Information overload means that apparently efficient means of communication can soon become unreliable. In 1994, Swedish Prime Minister Carl Bildt sent an e-mail to President Clinton, the first Internet exchange of its type. However, as the President receives up to 2,000 e-mails a day, the message was missed. After two days, Stockholm rang Washington.[28]

There is a compelling argument that information technology allows for extremely dense communications networks, so that it is difficult for one group to maintain a privileged source of information and inefficient for them to do so. It has also been argued that this will support networking-type organisations, while making life difficult for other, more hierarchical, forms. This is said to favour irregular warfare, as it helps dispersed and perhaps quite small groups to co-ordinate their activities, even without any formal organisation. The lack of central leadership means that a 'decapitation' attack is impossible. This can also be turned into an argument for flatter organisational structures in Western armed forces.

This type of organisation can probably only work when there is an underlying social cohesion or an attachment to a clear campaign objective, which can bring diverse individuals together. The supposition is that fighting networks, rather than hierarchies, involves facing a 'swarm' coming in from different angles and with different forms of attack, rather than a direct offensive.[29] This is similar to a guerrilla strategy, except that such strategies normally envisage a point at which dispersed units are strong enough to come together in a final bid to seize power. It is difficult to see how any group can move beyond making a nuisance of itself if it lacks an authoritative point of decision.

While there is no doubt that the information revolution puts an added burden on senior decision-makers, because the decision processes and their consequences will be much more transparent, it still tends to encourage centralised rather than dispersed decision-making. Initial conclusions from the Army's Task Force XXI suggest that, not surprisingly, it is much easier to be aware of the situation of friendly forces than that of enemy positions, that horizontal integration is not as smooth as vertical integration, which is more useful to a high commander than to those at the point of contact, and that the power requirements of keeping dismounted infantry plugged into the large network are extremely high.[30] As policy-makers have come to appreciate the costs and difficulties of this undertaking, Task Force XXI has become something much more transitional, preparing the way for the 'Army after Next'.[31]

The centralising tendency in the RMA may encourage micro-management by senior political leaders.[32] When everyone can talk to everyone else with equal facility, final decisions may well rise to points well beyond the level of competence. If commanders on the spot are to be allowed to exercise their own initiative, those above them will need to show great self-restraint.

Identifying the appropriate level of command is not always straightforward. Lieutenant-Colonel Dennis Murphy has noted the phenomenon of the 'strategic soldier', pointing out how a Marine platoon leader involved in a firefight in Haiti, a dead Ranger dragged through the streets of Mogadishu and a pilot downed over Bosnia have 'spurred National Command Authority involvement'.[33] In circumstances where small engagements can have large strategic consequences, it is important that the political implications of apparently tactical decisions are appreciated, yet an attempt to exercise too tight a control over small but complicated incidents can have distorting effects.

Even if 'perfect' information offers numerous targets, priorities will still have to be set. If they have to change suddenly because of new information, the consequences could be serious in a system expected to be so efficient that there are few margins of error. The line between 'just in time' and 'just too late' in scheduling and delivery may be a thin one. Moreover, questions of resource allocation become more difficult when there are horizontal as well as vertical lines of communication. If it is the case that a small ground unit can call in a cruise missile or a stealth bomber, more senior commanders will be even more anxious to ensure that this power is being used wisely and efficiently than if units were essentially reliant upon their own resources.

The difficulties can be illustrated by reference to a paper by David Alberts. Alberts writes enthusiastically of moving from decision-making 'under "uncertainty" or in the presence of incomplete and erroneous information' to a situation in which 'decisions are made with near "perfect" information'.[34] As published, this sentence contained two proof-reading errors ('erroneous' as 'erroneously' and 'made' as 'make'), illustrating the problems of achieving perfection in the transmission of information, especially when fallible human beings are involved.

It is important to distinguish between the ease with which a decision is made and its quality. Good and timely information is always welcome, but it will never be complete. High-speed, analytical systems may drive decision-takers towards certain kinds of decision, without sufficient regard for factors which may not be readily quantifiable, such as the morale of forces, the demands of allies, the mood in the UN, the state of domestic opinion and the economic implications of resources being expended at a particular rate.

The problems could be even worse if unreal expectations have been created for the informational aspects of war, so that disorientation may result from an interruption to the data flow. Friction may result simply because the reality facing units in battle is so different from the 'cyberworld' of simulations and war-gaming.[35] It would be foolish to argue against reaping the benefits of the information revolution, so long as they are kept on tap, rather than on top.

Once it is recognised that few conflicts are resolved in a culminating, decisive battle, the more important these other factors become. The relative importance of intelligence, for example, may be at its greatest in operations against militias, terrorists or criminals, when the availability of overwhelming force is rarely the problem. Such groups rely on deception and concealment in an effort to gain surprise for their operations. The sort of 'battlespace knowledge' required for an imminent clash of regular forces may be less helpful when tracking the furtive terrorist or the stealthy militia-member. In the latter cases, it may be 'softer', rather than 'harder', data that is required, which can only be interpreted through a keen sense of local culture and politics. The opponents may not have recognisable 'signatures', limiting the value of surveillance. Rather than being linked to precision weapons, intelligence may have to be linked to foot patrols or special operations. 'Dominant situational awareness' will need to take in broad economic, social and political developments as well as the order of battle.

## chapter 5

# Americans and Allies

## The Information Revolution and US Power

The Cold War was resolved through information warfare, a consequence of the vulnerability of closed societies to open communications. Many of the early advances in communication, such as the radio, were seen as natural instruments of totalitarianism. Radio released individuals from dependence upon local sources of knowledge, thereby diminishing at a stroke traditional sources of authority and creating a 'mass society' reliant on externally generated news which could be controlled by a central authority. The masses need hear only one voice, and this voice would be inescapable. This same central authority would be able to monitor loose talk and subversive action. This was the grim vision of George Orwell's *1984*. Big Brother controlled the information environment. It did not work out that way because no country could ever be sealed off from external influences.

The use of satellites to gather information was recognised in the 1960s as a challenge to Soviet military secrecy. They could photograph military establishments with impunity. They could chart every inch of Soviet territory, mocking those maps with built-in errors designed to confuse an invading force. The nearest the Soviet leadership ever came to justifying an anti-satellite system was in connection with its fear of direct broadcasting from space. The most vulnerable points of the Soviet system turned out to be its inability to jam completely the BBC World Service, or to prevent the intrusion into Soviet and East European homes of Western television programmes that undermined the official line simply by demonstrating an alternative, freer, more prosperous way of life. This did not require any overt political message.

Keeping a society sealed off from external influences is not becoming any easier. Even before the Internet, new forms of communication were giving rise to new forms of subversive action as part of the search to disseminate political messages and avoid censorship. Thus, audio tapes were used during the 1978 overthrow of the Shah of Iran, videotapes in the mid-1980s Philippine Revolution and fax machines in the campaign against General Manuel Noriega in the late 1970s.[1] When the Mexican government moved against the Zapatistas in the 1990s, the rebels used laptops to issue commands and the Internet to publicise allegations of government atrocities to gain support from international organisations. In national politics, e-mail campaigns of harassment have been devised and these can be extended internationally. The possibilities grow with the ease of transmission of video and audio material through the Internet.

China bans satellite receivers as it struggles to combine the communications demands of the global economy with the Communist Party's desperation to maintain a monopoly of political power. Singapore seeks to establish controls over the Internet to prevent the movement of unauthorised political messages as well as pornography, and Myanmar is trying to prevent any 'surfing' at all. Saudi Arabia has been vexed by its inability to stop dissident faxes being sent from London.

These examples encourage the view that the information revolution is a friend of open societies. This does not, however, mean that it has transformed the nature of international power. Joseph Nye and William Owen, two of the more optimistic proponents of the RMA, argue that technology, education and institutional flexibility are growing in importance compared to such traditional measures of strength as gross national product (GNP), military force, population, energy, land, and minerals. According to Nye and Owen:

> *The one country that can best lead the information revolution*
> *will be more powerful than any other. For the foreseeable*
> *future, that country is the United States.*[2]

Claims of this sort must be treated with care. The importance of the information revolution lies not in the accumulation of knowledge for its own sake, but in its impact on established forms of economic and military strength. Information is not a commodity that can be compared with land, minerals or wealth. It is the ultimate renewable resource, often in forms so accessible that they cannot be monopolised. Systems for processing information are becoming more sophisticated and also widely available.

The formidable strengths of the US can be traced to the advantages of its location, the vibrancy of its political system, the dynamism of its economy and the military firepower at its disposal. Its success in managing the information revolution may have enhanced those strengths, but offers no substitute for them. Nye and Owen's claim that, as a result of 'dominant battlespace knowledge', the US will 'be able to prevail militarily, whether the arena is triple-canopy jungle, an urban area or similar to Desert Storm' is also doubtful.[3] US military power reflects the size of its armed forces and the quality of personnel and training. The 'information difference' matters because of the raw material upon which it can work. The main question is not overall US capacity, which on all pertinent measures remains impressive, but its application in practice and its relevance to the challenges of the coming decades. 'Dominant battlespace knowledge' may be irrelevant if there is a marked absence of battlespaces in the future. At issue is the role the US expects to play in the world. The key factor shaping the character of future conventional war will be whether or not the US is directly engaged.

If RMA-type forces prove to be of only limited value in everyday international affairs, they are unlikely to provide the basis for a new international hierarchy. It is no longer the case that even raw military strength is now respected as an indicator of comparative political power. In the past, listing the most prominent platforms gave them unwarranted salience at the expense of the many other, often more intangible, elements of a military capability such as logistical competence and the quality of doctrine, morale and training. There is much to be said for the view that these questionable, traditional measures of the military balance have been rendered even more dubious because of the growing importance of weapons and information systems as against platforms.[4] Although it is possible to set an RMA standard against which the capacities of countries might be assessed, the real difficulty is that military power can only be truly judged against the political purposes it is intended to serve.[5]

## Consequences for Force Structures

The build-up in military equipment that began in the 1980s means that the basic parameters of the force structures of most Western countries, including the US, have already been set. It is not until this relatively new equipment begins to wear out, around 2010–20, that there will be an opportunity to impose radical new changes, although many transitional changes can be implemented before that date. Hence, the complaint that the dead-weight of 'legacy' programmes is squeezing out the 'vanguard' programmes. The report of the 1997 National Defense Panel argued strongly that the pace of change was not fast enough and needed to be accelerated.[6]

Even with a more focused approach, innovation will still be expensive. For this reason, there will be a search for cheap alternatives to expensive platforms for simpler missions. High-quality systems will be fitted to established platforms for the more demanding missions. Some platforms may never be replaced in kind but, through upgrading, will still play prominent roles. In the context of the current preoccupation with futuristic systems, it is remarkable that the USAF has even considered retaining the B-52H strategic bomber in service until 2045, an in-service span of almost a century.[7]

Consider, for example, the anticipated switch from manned aircraft to UAVs for purposes of reconnaissance, surveillance and electronic warfare. This has been anticipated for some time, since the first remotely piloted vehicles were introduced during the Vietnam War. A series of technical and reliability problems led to disappointment. Now there is more confidence that these have been overcome, but the equipment they carry to make them comparable with a manned aircraft's capabilities can still render them extremely expensive. The cost of the US *Global Hawk*, for example, designed to operate at high altitudes, has been put at $10m. The value of such a system is

*can there be selective RMA?*

heavily dependent upon its overall reliability, ability to survive in hostile airspace and the data-processing systems that can interpret and disseminate information quickly.[8]

The new technologies have important implications for industrial policy. The old defence industry was based on dedicated programmes with only a limited civilian spin-off. This now exists side by side with a more dynamic industry, which can pass through two generations of technology while the official defence-procurement machinery is still working its way laboriously through its bureaucratic mechanisms. Although the electronics and computing sectors originally took off on the back of military investment, they have now developed their civilian markets to such an extent that even the US military is a minor player. They also think globally and do not organise their business structures with national security in mind. A number may not even be that interested in defence contracts, for these tend to have low margins, slow decision-making and procurement processes and an onerous regulatory framework. On the other hand, these companies do take corporate security seriously, and this includes keeping up to date and alert on many of the areas associated with information warfare. Thus, in buying off the shelf, it may be possible to secure 80% of the capability, including sensitivity to a number of potential vulnerabilities. The choice that military establishments will increasingly need to make is whether the extra 20% of capability is worth the possible 80% of extra investment and the delays required for dedicated military systems. It seems likely that, in the future, the onus will be on procurement agencies to demonstrate why they should not buy off the shelf.

The RMA also has critical personnel implications. It requires software specialists and educated operators – exactly those areas where there is high demand for qualified personnel from the most energetic sections of the civilian economy. Couple this with the intensive manpower demands of many of the smaller-scale contingencies and it is possible to see the cost of volunteer forces growing significantly, again reducing the capacity for longer-term investments. This argues for an imaginative approach to reserve forces given that information-technology skills are now widespread in civilian life. Making room for more experimental research and testing will require the US to show a greater readiness to close bases and reduce established forces than has been shown up to now.

## Can Non-Americans Keep Up?

It is almost impossible to identify any country or group of countries that would have the resources to match the US in RMA capabilities, even if inclined to do so. Russia has become increasingly dependent upon its nuclear strength to maintain any sort of great-power status. It will take many years to move to a smaller, volunteer force with advanced conventional capabilities. China is modernising its armed forces, but from a very low base, although, as to be expected from the land of Sun Tzu, it has shown an interest in information operations as compensation for weaknesses elsewhere in its force structure.[9] The countries best able to follow the US are its leading West European and Asia-Pacific allies, but they also suffer from severe resource constraints and other important demands on the military budget.

The challenge for many countries will be to identify that level of extra capability that is worth a dedicated military investment rather than a much cheaper adaptation of programmes under development for the civilian market. While some capabilities for intelligence, communication and targeting are becoming widely accessible, others remain highly specialist and at a degree of sophistication that is unavailable outside the higher military sphere, including the most advanced forms of systems integration. In general, there will be hybrid conventional capabilities, acquired selectively and in an uneven and unco-ordinated manner.

In many armed forces, again perhaps including those of the US, two tiers might develop, with one tier geared to advanced warfare while the other, with fewer resources and less well-equipped, would be left to cope with residual, more mundane, but also more likely contingencies. This gap may well be evident within an alliance or 'coalition of the willing', leading to awkward debates on the distribution of roles and missions.

Any limits on the acquisition of advanced systems are unlikely to have much to do with attempts at international regulation of the relevant markets. Cruise missiles, for example, are to some extent the paradigmatic weapon of the RMA, as delivery systems that can be launched from a variety of platforms and strike in a precise manner and with low collateral damage. They have also proliferated significantly, especially in the form of anti-ship missiles.

The Missile Technology Control Regime (MTCR) seeks to constrain, through a common export policy, UAVs capable of delivering a payload of 500kg over at least 300km. By 1998, it took in 29 states, and includes all systems able to carry chemical, nuclear or conventional weapons. Although it has made an important contribution with regard to ballistic missiles, there are limits to how far this can be extended towards cruise missiles. The regime cannot cope with aircraft

*the limits of arms control*

– and many components of cruise missiles are similar to those of aircraft.[10] In July 1996, 33 nations signed the Wassenaar Arrangement on Export Controls for Conventional Arms and Dual-Use Goods and Technologies. Unfortunately, this has no teeth and is, according to William Keller and Janne Nolan, 'languishing', having 'received scant attention from the policy community and ridicule from the arms lobby'.[11]

Most RMA-type technologies can neither be readily counted nor verified, and therefore do not fit into any of the traditional sorts of arms-control agreements. The point has already been made about the consequences of the 'civilianisation' of the many important forms of information collection and transmission. In this area, only some of the more esoteric electronic counter-measures and counter-counter-measures may be kept from general release. During the Cold War, one of the roles for arms control was to confirm an international power structure. For this reason, agreements tended towards a general accounting exercise.

## Relations with Allies

The US might be able to extend RMA-type deterrence to its allies to persuade others that there is little point in confronting the West in a conventional battle. The problem lies with those conflicts that cannot be readily deterred, and are unlikely to be responsive to RMA-type operations. If the US decides not to become involved, it might still provide logistics, intelligence and air power. As in the Iran–Iraq War, the provision of high-grade intelligence might be used to 'tilt' a conflict in the preferred direction. Allies may be less enthusiastic if similar provision comes to define the US contribution to operations that are being conducted in pursuit of a wider Western, or international, interest.

Nye and Owen suggest that the US could use its 'information dominance' to back up the forces of local allies. Making 'situational awareness' available would obviate the need for them to purchase their own 'system of systems'.[12] Libicki also writes of how the US could 'supply the information that would permit them to use smart munitions to approach near-perfect kill probabilities'.[13] Providing the 'situational awareness' and the targeting guidance for others has obvious attractions from a US perspective. If there is too much of a gap between US capabilities and those of its allies, however, the US will not even be able to bestow these benefits because the recipients will be unable to take advantage of them. If the problems with interoperability are manageable, few belligerents are likely to turn away what is on offer, even if it is less than ideal. There would be the normal discomfort about being so reliant upon a power that was not totally committed to battle and following its own agenda.

The salient aspects of a situation can appear quite different from the perspective of a spectator than from centre stage. As was seen during the earlier stages of the Bosnian conflict, resentments can soon build up when it appears that the US is advising, and even pressuring, allies to take certain risks with their forces that it is not prepared to take with its own. Given the centralising nature of the 'system of systems', there could be concern that Washington was in effective charge, even when its own liabilities in a situation were strictly limited. Nor would the allies relish the role of 'spear-carriers', helping to create the appearance of a coalition to demonstrate that the US is acting on behalf of more than unilateral interest, yet deemed inadequate when it comes to participating in the most technologically demanding roles.

For all these reasons, few are likely to accept in advance dependence upon US systems even when, at times of crisis, they have little choice but to do so. The most important allies of the US will make an effort to stay abreast of these technologies and to adopt them where possible, if only for purposes of interoperability and to gain access to US policy-making at times of crisis and war. It will become the subscription to be taken seriously as an ally.

# The Revolution in Strategic Affairs

The official US position is that forces optimised for large-scale conventional war should be able to accomplish other tasks. Thus, *Joint Vision 2010*, the 'template' for the evolution of the US armed forces, seeks to build on the country's 'core strengths of high quality people and information-age technological advances' by developing four operational concepts – 'dominant maneuver, precision engagement, full dimensional protection, and focused logistics'. It claims that the application of these concepts will provide 'Full Spectrum Dominance' – a capability to 'dominate an opponent across the range of military operations'.[1] Maintaining large wars as a priority assumes, as the National Defense Panel puts it, that the current, relatively calm international environment may be no more than an 'interlude'. Eventually, a serious 'peer competitor' will emerge, ready to challenge the benign hegemony of the US. The penalties could be severe if investment for this moment has been neglected because a distracting preoccupation with 'recent trends in civil disturbance' has led to a chase after minor irritants.[2]

This sort of deterioration in the strategic environment would arise not only as a result of a failure in military investment, but also one of political investment. A major confrontation at some distant date is most likely to be avoided if constant attention is paid to supporting and consolidating the more positive aspects of the current international scene. The neglect of the small-scale contingencies may increase the probability of the large scale. In the first instance, reducing general levels of violence and preventing the aggravation of regional conflicts depends on imaginative diplomacy, but this may well need to be backed up by military force. On this assumption, it would be unwise to consider the relatively small-scale – but quite regular – contingencies as being secondary and residual on the off-chance that there might be a very large-scale contingency in a couple of decades.[3] This secondary character is reflected in the designation 'Military Operations Other Than War' (MOOTW), a term which replaced the equally misleading 'low-intensity conflict'. These operations certainly have a warlike quality.[4]

Instead of being viewed as 'lesser-included cases', it is important to appreciate the special demands, in terms of equipment mixes, training and rules of engagement, made by these smaller-scale contingencies.[5] These contingencies can arise out of conflicts of all shapes and sizes. They point to areas where size measured in terms of input (commitments of regular armed forces) may have little relation to that of output (social impact), and which are highly political in all their aspects. In terms of time, the demands of coalition-building, with negotiations over objectives, rules of engagement and burden-sharing, will affect the speed with which an operation can be mounted, while the demands of stability support will require a presence to be sustained over an extended period. In terms of space, most operations will be conducted some distance from home. This means that they will be expeditionary in character, relying on whatever forces are available, and putting a great stress on logistics.[6] An activist approach will therefore require the despatch of naval task forces to areas of crisis, plus overseas bases and pre-positioned stores to allow for quick response times and reduced dependence on awkward logistics chains.

The combination of preponderant military power with limited political ambition apparently allows the US the strategic luxury of being able to design future wars largely according to its own preferences. Should a particular conflict fail to match the template, Washington can choose not to become involved. There is a potential competition for resources here. If too much effort is put into RMA technologies, then the numbers of platforms and weapons could fall, perhaps to the point where there is no longer a critical mass for certain types of forces and basic manpower requirements cannot be met. This, it should be said, is much more likely to be a problem for its allies than for the US itself. Most of the roles for which armed forces must prepare in most parts of the world require infantry. This is the case whenever the problem is one of civic order, whether at home, in an adjacent territory or overseas. For many roles, where 'presence' is important, forces must be conspicuous, even if they are not that capable. An attempt to develop the 'system of systems' could, by itself, account for perhaps up to a third of a defence budget.

The tension between these demands on forces and the development of RMA-type capabilities should not be overstated. In principle, many features of the RMA are relevant to smaller-scale contingencies, especially with intelligence and surveillance and in making possible more selective use of artillery and air power. It makes sense for those capabilities with the widest possible application, such as precision weapons and $C^4I$ capabilities, to be the priority areas for future investment.[7] Furthermore, for all forms of future combat, there is a strong case for reducing the size of the normal operational unit (brigades rather than divisions, squadrons rather than wings and smaller battle groups).[8]

The current US investment in conventional capabilities will not be used at anything approaching full stretch because countries will go to considerable lengths to avoid this sort of engagement. The revolution of expectations caused by the Gulf War means that the implications of taking on the US in a conventional confrontation are well understood. This is hardly a trivial matter as the deterrent effect already is considerable. Just because a capability is not used does not render it irrelevant. Nuclear weapons have not been used in anger since 1945, but their existence has had profound strategic consequences. They helped to ensure that certain wars were not fought, and that others were kept more limited than might otherwise have been the case.

This paper is concerned with the realism of the prospect of relatively civilised warfare offered by the RMA, unsullied by either the destructiveness of nuclear war or the murky, subversive character of terrorism or militia-type wars, of professional war conducted by professional armies – the vision, in A. C. Bacevich's sardonic words, 'of the Persian Gulf War replayed over and over again'.[9] At issue here is not the relevance of many of the systems now associated with the RMA. It is hard to imagine any conflict in which Western forces are involved in which commanders will not want to acquire and exploit the best information, target their forces with precision and keep casualties to a minimum. The problem lies in the extent to which opponents will fight in the same way.

The conduct of hostilities since the Second World War has, as often as not, represented a tradition of war-fighting. Guerrilla operations and terrorism have also shown increasing sophistication and ingenuity. In many recent conflicts, chemical weapons, ballistic missiles or simply any means at hand that can kill large numbers of people have been employed. The Western Way of Warfare, reinforced by the RMA, points to operations initiated before those of opponents, stand-off weapons rather than organic firepower making possible a more limited role for ground forces, reduced dependence on logistics, quick and unequivocal results, and a sharp distinction between combatants and non-combatants. Yet against this must be set the tendency towards conflicts involving complex interactions with the civil societies of all participants, working against attempts to maintain a sharp differentiation between combatants and non-combatants.

Policy-makers are properly put on their guard by attempts to dazzle them with exotic systems that promise a future radically different from the present. They are more likely to be alienated than enthused. Douglas Lovelace observes that the sudden introduction of concepts such as 'pop up warfare', 'fire ant warfare' and 'nano-technology' provided very little that policy-makers could relate to in their 'contemporary decision-making needs'.[10] In practice, the revolution in strategic affairs is driven less by the pace of technological change than by uncertainties in political conditions. Military planners must consider potential enemies from fanatical terrorists to disaffected great powers. They must prepare for hostile acts, which can cover the spectrum from the improvised explosive device in a shopping mall to guerrilla ambushes to traditional battle to nuclear exchanges, and perhaps even 'cyberwar' directed against critical information systems.

The permutations of enemies and modes of warfare are endless: terrorists might gain access to WMD, renegade states might plant bombs in public places, a mischievous hacker might insinuate himself into the computer networks of a country's military establishment, while drug cartels might arm themselves for pitched battles. Governments require a set of capabilities that can provide the flexibility and versatility to cope with this wide range of contingencies. The more warfare becomes intermingled with normal civilian activity, whether as militias rather than regular forces, international criminal networks developing their own armies or military intelligence being gathered using commercially available systems, the more difficult it is to respond by conventional military means.

There is thus a contrast between the trend towards the isolation of Western military organisations – manned only by volunteers and determined to confine hostilities to combatants on both sides – from the wider society, and the social character of the more likely conflicts. It fits in with the assumption that, for the moment at least, Western countries can choose their enemies and are not obliged to fight on anybody else's terms. Invitations to war need only be accepted on certain conditions: public opinion must be supportive; the result must be pre-ordained; and the conflict must be structured as a contest between highly professional conventional forces. Military commanders must devise strategies that not only keep their own casualty levels low, but also respect the expectation – bordering on a moral presumption – that fire will be directed with precision and only against targets of evident military value.

Such views are suitable for political entities that are not fearful, desperate, vengeful or angry and that can maintain a sense of proportion over the interests at stake and the humanity of the opponent. They are not necessarily the views of those whom Western states might confront in combat. They reflect, to an extent, an a priori detachment from the wellsprings of conflict and violence in the modern world, the perspective of a concerned observer rather than a committed participant. The sense of proper restraint when it comes to employing armed force may be profound and deeply felt, but it is also conditional and can break down in circumstances of political turmoil. While the technology of armed force and its forms of organisation may change, its use or invocation still excites emotions and passions that are timeless. Its influence on political events still depends on an actual or demonstrable capacity to damage life and property.

There would be reasons for relief if belligerents only targeted information flows. Unfortunately, it is as likely that they will turn to any methods of causing hurt in an effort to encourage a sense of disproportion in the population and unhinge multilateral coalitions. The RMA does not offer the prospect of a virtual war by creating a situation in which only information matters so that there is never any point in fighting about anything other than information. Territory, prosperity, identity, order, values – they all still matter, and provide the ultimate tests of a war's success. War is not a virtual thing, played out on screens, but intensely physical. That is why it tends to violence and destruction. The response in the West to this prospect may be to become even less activist, to avoid becoming involved in conflicts that carry a high risk of turning into the wrong sort of war. It will, however, hardly be a revolution in military affairs if it leads those who embrace it to avoid most contemporary conflicts, and only to take on those that promise the certain and relatively painless victories.

## Acknowledgements

The author would like to thank Dr François Heisbourg, Sir Peter Hill-Norton, Sir Michael Quinlan and Dr Andrew Rathmell for their advice and comments.

## Introduction

[1] Williamson Murray, 'Thinking About Revolutions in Military Affairs', *Joint Force Quarterly*, no. 16, Summer 1997, p. 69.

[2] Douglas MacGregor, *Breaking the Phalanx: A New Design for Landpower in the 21st Century* (Westport, CT: Praeger Publishers, 1997), p. 141.

[3] On the different versions of the RMA, see Colin Gray, 'The American Revolution in Military Affairs: An Interim Assessment', *The Occasional*, no. 28, Strategic and Combat Studies Institute (SCSI), September 1997.

[4] Andrew Krepinevich, 'Cavalry to Computer: The Pattern of Military Revolutions', *The National Interest*, no. 37, Autumn 1994, p. 30.

[5] William Lind et al., 'The Changing Face of War: Into the Fourth Generation', *Military Review*, vol. 69, no. 10, October 1989. This reflects views also associated with Martin van Creveld. See van Creveld, *The Transformation of War* (New York: The Free Press, 1991).

[6] Alvin and Heidi Toffler, *War and Anti-War: Survival at the Dawn of the 21st Century* (Boston, MA: Little Brown & Co, 1993).

[7] For a critique, see Kenneth McKenzie, 'Elegant Irrelevance: Fourth Generation Warfare', *Parameters*, vol. 23, no. 3, Autumn 1992–93, pp. 51–60.

## Chapter 1

[1] Admiral William Owens, 'The Emerging System of Systems', *US Naval Institute Proceedings*, vol. 121, no. 5, May 1995, pp. 35–39.

[2] Mark Hanna, 'Task Force XXI: The Army's Digital Experiment', *Strategic Forum*, no. 119, July 1997.

[3] Ben Lambeth, 'The Technology

Revolution in Air Warfare', *Survival*, vol. 39, no. 1, Spring 1997, p. 72; John A. Warden III, 'The Enemy as a System', *Airpower Journal*, vol. 9, no. 1, Spring 1995, pp. 40–55.

[4] Douglas MacGregor, 'Future Battle: The Merging Levels of War', *Parameters*, vol. 22, no. 4, Winter 1992–93, p. 42.

[5] Martin Libicki, 'DBK and its Consequences', in Stuart Johnson and Martin Libicki (eds), *Dominant Battlespace Knowledge* (Washington DC: National Defense University, 1996), p. 18.

[6] James Hazlett, 'Just-In-Time Warfare', in *ibid.*, p. 116.

[7] Basil Liddell Hart, 'Continental Victories or Economic Pressure', *Journal of the Royal United Services Institute*, 1931.

[8] Basil Liddell Hart, *The Revolution in Warfare* (London: Faber & Faber Limited, 1946).

[9] Edward Luttwak, 'A Post-Heroic Military Policy', *Foreign Affairs*, vol. 75, no. 4, July–August 1996, pp. 33–44.

[10] *Joint Military Net Assessment* (Washington DC: Department of Defense, 1993), p. 3. Quoted in Keith Payne, 'Post-Cold War Deterrence and Missile Defense', *Orbis*, vol. 39, no. 2, Spring 1995, p. 203.

[11] Chris Morris, Janet Morris and Thomas Baines, 'Weapons of Mass Protection: Nonlethality, Information Warfare and Airpower in the Age of Chaos', *Airpower Journal*, vol. 9, no. 1, Spring 1995, p. 15.

[12] Colonel Martin Stanton, 'What Price Sticky Foam', *US Naval Institute Proceedings*, vol. 122, no. 1, January 1996, p. 59. Cited in Nick Lewer and Steven Schofield, *Non-Lethal Weapons: A Fatal Attraction?* (London: Zed Books, 1997), p. 129.

## Chapter 2

[1] V. D. Sokolovskiy, *Soviet Military Strategy*, 3rd Edition (London: MacDonald and Jane's, 1975) contains a number of references to this revolution. In her introduction (p. xx), the US editor of this translation, Harriet Fast Scott, suggests that for Soviet strategists this revolution had taken place by 1960.

[2] Richard Burt, 'The Cruise Missile and Arms Control', *Survival*, vol. 18, no. 1, January–February 1976, pp. 10–17.

[3] Alain Enthoven and Wayne Smith, *How Much is Enough: Shaping the Defense Program 1961–1969* (London: Harper & Row, 1971). Michael McGwire, *Military Objectives in Soviet Foreign Policy* (Washington DC: Brookings Institution, 1987).

[4] Colonel John Warden, *The Air Campaign: Planning for Combat* (Washington DC: National Defense University, 1988).

[5] Mark Clodfelter, *The Limits of Air Power: The American Bombing of North Vietnam* (New York: The Free Press, 1989).

[6] Richard Burt, *New Weapons Technologies: Debate and Directions*, Adelphi Paper 126 (London: IISS, 1976), p. 3.

[7] Malcolm Currie, *Statement to the House Appropriations Committee: Department of Defense Appropriations for 1975* (Washington DC: US Government Printing Office (USGPO), 1974), Part 4, p. 450. Cited in Burt, *New Weapons Technologies*, p. 2.

[8] Caspar Weinberger,

*Standardization of Equipment within NATO: Tenth Report to the US Congress* (Washington DC: Department of Defense, 1984), p. 1. Cited in John Roper, 'Technological Development and Force Structure Within the Western Alliance: Prospects for Rationalisation and Division of Labour: Part II', in *New Technology and Western Security*, Part I, Adelphi Paper 197 (London: IISS, 1985), p. 51.

[9] Seymour Deitchman, 'Weapons, Platforms and the New Armed Services', *Issues in Science and Technology*, vol. 1, no. 3, Spring 1985.

[10] European Security Study, *Strengthening Conventional Deterrence* (New York: St Martin's Press, 1983).

[11] Ingemar Dörfer, 'Technological Development and Force Structure Within the Western Alliance: Prospects for Rationalisation and Division of Labour: Part I', in *New Technology and Western Security*, Part I, p. 39. See also the lukewarm essay in the British government's *1983 Statement on the Defence Estimates* (London: Her Majesty's Stationery Office (HMSO), 1983).

[12] Henri Conze, 'Conventional Force Development and New Technology: How Real are the Gains in Prospect?', in *New Technology and Western Security*, Part II, p. 6.

[13] William Lind, 'Some Doctrinal Questions for the United States Army', *Military Review*, March 1977, pp. 54–65.

[14] Edward Luttwak, 'The Operational Level of War', *International Security*, vol. 5, no. 3, Winter 1980–81, pp. 61–79.

[15] Army Field Manual FM-100-5, *Operations* (Washington DC: USGPO, 1982). See Lieutenant-Colonel Huba Wass de Czege and Lieutenant-Colonel L. D. Holder, 'The New FM 100-5', *Military Review*, vol. 62, no. 7, July 1982.

[16] Joint Pub. 3.0, *Doctrine for Joint Operations* (Washington DC: USGPO, 1993), cited in David Jablonsky, 'US Military Doctrine and the Revolution in Military Affairs', *Parameters*, vol. 24, no. 3, Autumn 1994, pp. 18–36.

[17] John Mearsheimer, 'Maneuver, Mobile Defense, and the NATO Central Front', *International Security*, vol. 6, no. 3, Winter 1981–82.

[18] James Fallows, *National Defense* (New York: Random House, 1981).

[19] William Lind, 'A Doubtful Revolution', *Issues in Science and Technology*, vol. 1, no. 3, Spring 1985. This was in response to Deitchman's essay discussed above.

[20] Steven Canby, 'New Conventional Force Technology and the NATO–Warsaw Pact Balance: Part I', in *New Technology and Western Security*, Part II, p. 7.

[21] *Ibid.*, p. 8.

[22] Stephen J. Blank, 'Preparing for the Next War: Reflections on the Revolution in Military Affairs', *Strategic Review*, vol. 24, no. 2, Spring 1996, pp. 20–21; 'The Soviet Strategic View: Ogarkov on the Revolution in Military Technology', *ibid.*, vol. 12, no. 3, Summer 1984.

[23] John P. Holdren, 'SDI, the Soviets, and the Prospects for Arms Control', in Sanford Lakoff and Randy Willoughby (eds), *Strategic Defense and the Western Alliance* (Lexington, MA: Lexington Books, 1987), p. 197.

24 Barry D. Watts, 'Effects and Effectiveness', in Eliot A. Cohen (ed.), *Gulf War Air Power Survey, Vol. 2, Operations and Effects and Effectiveness* (Washington DC: USGPO, 1993), p. 363.

25 Alan Campen (ed.), *The First Information War: The Story of Communications, Computers, and Intelligence Systems in the Persian Gulf War* (Fairfax, VA: AFCEA International Press, 1992); Edward Mann, 'Desert Storm: The First Information War?', *Airpower Journal*, vol. 8, no. 4, Winter 1994, pp. 4–14; Steven Lambakis, 'The World's First Space War', *Orbis*, vol. 39, no. 3, Summer 1995, pp. 417–33. The same idea is found in the title of Sir Peter Anson and Dennis Cummings, 'The First Space War: The Contribution of Satellites to the Gulf War', *Journal of the Royal United Services Institute*, vol. 136, no. 4, Winter 1991, pp. 45–53.

26 See the table 'The Space Order of Battle in Desert Storm', in Anthony H. Cordesman and Abraham R. Wagner, *The Lessons of Modern War, Volume 4: The Gulf War* (Boulder, CO: Westview Press, 1995), p. 259. This is largely adapted from David Tretler and Daniel T. Kuehl, 'A Statistical Compendium', in Eliot A. Cohen (ed.), *Gulf War Air Power Survey, Vol. 5, A Statistical Compendium and Chronology* (Washington DC: USGPO, 1993), pp. 126–32.

27 Michael Russell Rip and David P. Lusch, 'The Precision Revolution: The Navstar Global Positioning System in the Second Gulf War', *Intelligence and National Security*, vol. 9, no. 2, April 1994, pp. 167–241.

28 Theodore A. Postal, 'Lessons of the Gulf War Experience with Patriot', *International Security*, vol. 16, no. 3, Winter 1991–92, pp. 119–71.

29 Cordesman and Wagner, *The Lessons of Modern War, Volume 4*, p. 238.

30 Barry D. Watts, *Clausewitzian Friction and Future War*, McNair Paper 52 (Washington DC: National Defense University, 1996).

31 Benjamin Lambeth, 'Bounding the Air Power Debate', *Strategic Review*, vol. 25, no. 4, Autumn 1994, pp. 42–55.

32 Department of Defense, *Conduct of the Persian Gulf War, Final Report to Congress* (Washington DC: USGPO, 1992), p. 164.

33 James Blackwell, Michael J. Mazarr and Don Snider, *The Gulf War: Military Lessons Learned* (Washington DC: Center for Strategic and International Studies (CSIS), 1991), p. 21. This was followed up with Michael J. Mazarr et al., *The Military Technical Revolution: A Structural Framework* (Washington DC: CSIS, 1993). An influential early study was Andrew Krepinevich, 'The Military–Technical Revolution: A Preliminary Assessment', unpublished manuscript, Office of Net Assessment, July 1992. See also Antulio J. Echevarria and John Shaw, 'The New Military Revolution: Post-Industrial Change', *Parameters*, vol. 22, no. 4, Winter 1992–93, pp. 70–79 and Dan Gouré, 'Is There a Military–Technical Revolution in America's Future', *Washington Quarterly*, vol. 16, no. 4, Autumn 1993, pp. 175–92. For an early sceptical voice, see Eric Arnett, 'Welcome to Hyperwar', *Bulletin of the Atomic Scientists*, vol. 49, no. 1, September 1992, pp. 15–21.

[34] Major Norman Davis, 'An Information-Based Revolution in Military Affairs', *Strategic Review*, vol. 24, no. 1, Winter 1996, p. 43.

## Chapter 3

[1] Samuel P. Huntington, 'The Clash of Civilizations', *Foreign Affairs*, vol. 72, no. 3, Summer 1993, pp. 22–49.
[2] Robert Caplan, 'The Coming Anarchy', *The Atlantic Monthly*, vol. 275, no. 2, February 1994, pp. 44–76.
[3] Defense Secretary Caspar Weinberger, speech at the National Press Club, Washington DC, 28 November 1984; Secretary of State George Shultz, speech at Yeshiva University, New York, 9 December 1984.
[4] See Christopher Gacek, *The Logic of Force: The Dilemma of Limited War in American Foreign Policy* (New York: Columbia University Press, 1994), p. 336.
[5] Colin Powell, 'US Forces: Challenges Ahead', *Foreign Affairs*, vol. 71, no. 5, Winter 1992, pp. 32–45.
[6] Kenneth Allard, *Command, Control and the Common Defense*, Revised Edition (Washington DC: National Defense University, 1996), p. 301.
[7] See citations in Douglas Lovelace Jr, *The Evolution of Military Affairs: Shaping the Future US Armed Forces* (Washington DC: National Defense University, 1997), p. 69.
[8] Andrew Mack, 'Why Big Countries Lose Small Wars: The Politics of Asymmetric Conflict', *World Politics*, vol. 26, no. 1, 1975, pp. 175–200.
[9] Ralph Peters, 'The New Warrior Class', *Parameters*, vol. 24, no. 2,

Summer 1994, p. 20.
[10] Larry Cable, *Conflict of Myths: The Development of American Counterinsurgency Doctrine and the Vietnam War* (New York: New York University Press, 1986).
[11] Earl H. Tilford Jr, 'The Revolution In Military Affairs: Prospects And Cautions', US Army War College Strategic Studies Institute (SSI), June 1995.
[12] Stephen Biddle, 'Victory Misunderstood: What the Gulf War Tells Us About the Future of Conflict', *International Security*, vol. 21, no. 2, Autumn 1996, pp. 139–79.
[13] Stephen Biddle and Robert Zirkle, 'Technology, Civil–Military Relations, and Warfare in the Developing World', *Journal of Strategic Studies*, vol. 19, no. 2, June 1996, pp. 171–212.
[14] Ralph Peters, 'Our Soldiers, Their Cities', *Parameters*, vol. 26, no. 1, Spring 1996, pp. 43–49.
[15] The National Defense Panel, 'Transforming Defense: National Security in the 21st Century', December 1997, p. 36.
[16] *Ibid.*, p. 15.
[17] Colonel James Lasswell, 'Wall to Wall', *Armed Forces Journal International*, vol. 136, no. 1, January 1998, pp. 36–39.
[18] Libicki, 'DBK and its Consequences', p. 35.
[19] *Ibid.*, pp. 46–47.
[20] See Lawrence Freedman, *Strategic Defence in the Nuclear Age*, Adelphi Paper 224 (London: IISS, 1987).
[21] Paul K. Davis, Richard L. Kugler and Richard J. Hillestad, *Strategic Issues and Options for the Quadrennial Defense Review* (Santa Monica, CA: RAND, 1997).
[22] Robert A. Manning, 'The Nuclear Age: The Next Chapter',

*Foreign Policy*, no. 109, Winter 1997–98, p. 71.

[23] Fred Iklé, 'The Next Lenin: On the Cusp of Truly Revolutionary Warfare', *The National Interest*, no. 47, Spring 1997, pp. 9–19.

[24] 'Nuclear Weapons First in Russia's Defence Policy', IISS, *Strategic Comments*, vol. 4, no. 1, January 1998.

[25] Walter Laquer, 'Postmodern Terrorism', *Foreign Affairs*, vol. 75, no. 5, September–October 1996, pp. 24–36.

[26] Richard K. Betts, 'The New Threat of Mass Destruction', *ibid.*, vol. 77, no. 1, January–February 1998, pp. 26–41. The study was US Congress Office of Technology Assessment, *Proliferation of Weapons of Mass Destruction: Assessing the Risks* (Washington DC: USGPO, 1993).

[27] Lawrence Freedman, 'Great Powers, Vital Interests and Nuclear Weapons', *Survival*, vol. 36, no. 4, Winter 1994, pp. 35–52.

[28] R. Jeffrey Smith, 'Clinton Orders Changes in Nuclear-War Strategy', *International Herald Tribune*, 8 December 1997, pp. 1, 10.

[29] William Arkin, 'Calculated Ambiguity: Nuclear Weapons and the Gulf War', *Washington Quarterly*, vol. 19, no. 4, Autumn 1996, pp. 3–8.

### Chapter 4

[1] Brian Fredericks, 'Information Warfare at the Crossroads', *Joint Force Quarterly*, no. 16, Summer 1997, pp. 97–103.

[2] Colonel Michael D. Starry and Lieutenant-Colonel Charles W. Arneson, 'FM 100-6: Information Operations', *Military Review*, vol. 76, no. 6, November–December 1996, pp. 3–15.

[3] Joint Chiefs of Staff, *Concept for Future Joint Operations*, pp. 35–41.

[4] Martin Libicki, 'What is Information Warfare?', *ACIS Paper No. 3*, National Defense University, August 1995.

[5] Dan Kuehl, 'Defining Information Power', *Strategic Forum*, no. 115, June 1997.

[6] William Broad, 'How Nosy Can a Person Get? Private Spy Satellite Up and Running', *International Herald Tribune*, 26 December 1997, pp. 1–3.

[7] Bill Gregory, 'Down to Earth', *Armed Forces Journal International*, vol. 135, no. 5, December 1997, p. 12.

[8] For an early discussion of these issues, see Ann Florini, 'The Opening Skies: Third Party Imaging Satellites and US Security', in *International Security*, vol. 13, no. 2, Autumn 1988, pp. 91–123. See also Michael Krepon, Peter Zimmerman, Leonard Spector and Mary Umberger (eds), *Commercial Observation Satellites and International Security* (New York: St Martin's Press, 1990); Vipin Gupta, 'New Satellite Images for Sale', *International Security*, vol. 20, no. 1, Summer 1995, pp. 94–125; Bhupendra Jasani, 'Could Civil Satellites Monitor Nuclear Tests?', *Space Policy*, vol. 2, no. 1, February 1995, pp. 31–40. See also Irving Lachow, 'The GPS Dilemma: Balancing Military Risks and Economic Benefits', *International Security*, vol. 20, no. 1, Summer 1995, pp. 126–48.

[9] Frances Cairncross, *The Death of Distance: How the Communications Revolution will Change our Lives* (London: Orion Business, 1997), p. 87.

[10] Major-General David L. Grange and Colonel James A. Kelley, 'Information Operations for the Ground Commander', *Military Review*, vol. 77, no. 2, March–April 1997, p. 5.

[11] Steven Lambakis, 'Exploiting Space Control', *Armed Forces Journal International*, vol. 134, no. 11, June 1997, pp. 42–46.

[12] 'The Importance of Military Space', *Air Force Magazine*, June 1975, p. 28.

[13] Air Force Scientific Advisory Board, 'New World Vistas: Air and Space Power for the 21st Century, Summary Volume', December 1995, pp. iii, 11, 46–48.

[14] Paul Mann, 'Cyber Threat Expands with Unchecked Speed', *Aviation Week and Space Technology*, vol. 145, no. 2, 8 July 1996, pp. 63–64.

[15] David Alexander, 'Information Warfare and the Digitised Battlefield', *Military Technology*, September 1995, pp. 57–64. Paul Evancoe and Mark Bentley, 'CVW – Computer Virus as a Weapon', *ibid.*, May 1994, pp. 38–40.

[16] Stephen Bowes, 'Information Warfare', *Armed Forces Journal International*, February 1998, pp. 30–31.

[17] Andrew Rathmell, 'Cyber-Terrorism: The Shape of Future Conflict?', *Journal of the Royal United Services Institute*, October 1997, pp. 40–46.

[18] Cited in Starry and Arneson, 'FM 100-6: Information Operations', p. 6.

[19] Richard Szafranski, 'Neocortical Warfare? The Acme of Skill', *Military Review*, vol. 74, no. 11, November 1994, pp. 41–55.

[20] The issues are discussed in a visionary manner in John Arquilla and David Ronfeldt, 'Cyberwar is Coming', *Comparative Strategy*, vol. 12, no. 2, April–June 1993, pp. 141–65 and in Roger Molander, Andrew Riddile and Peter Wilson, *Strategic Information Warfare: A New Face of War* (Santa Monica, CA: RAND, 1996). For cautionary essays on the dangers of over-playing concepts of strategic information warfare, see Martin Libicki, *Defending Cyberspace and Other Metaphors* (Washington DC: National Defense University, 1997).

[21] Paul Feaver, 'Blowback: Information Warfare and the Dynamics of Coercion', paper presented at the 1997 Annual Meeting of the American Political Science Association, Washington DC, 8 October 1997.

[22] Timothy L. Thomas, 'Deterring Information Warfare: A New Strategic Challenge', *Parameters*, vol. 26, no. 4, Winter 1996–97, p. 82. See also Thomas, 'The Threat of Information Operations; A Russian Perspective', in Robert Pfalzgraff Jr and Richard H. Shultz (eds), *War in the Information Age* (Washington DC: Brassey's, 1997), pp. 61–79.

[23] Michael May, 'War or Peace in Space', Discussion Paper No. 93, Californian Seminar on Arms Control and Foreign Policy, March 1981, pp. 7–8. Cited in Colin Gray, *American Military Space Policy* (London: Greenwood Press, 1996), p. 5.

[24] R. L. DiNardo and Daniel J. Hughes, 'Some Cautionary Thoughts on Information Warfare', *Airpower Journal*, vol. 9, no. 4, Winter 1995, p. 71.

[25] Mark McNeilly, *Sun Tzu and the Art of Business* (Oxford: Oxford University Press, 1996). The standard translation of Sun Tzu is

by Samuel B. Griffith. Sun Tzu, *The Art of War* (Oxford: Oxford University Press, 1971).
[26] Joint Chiefs of Staff, *Concept for Future Joint Operations* (Washington DC: Department of Defense, 1997), p. 35. The quote comes from *The Art of War*, p. 84. It is discussed, with Clausewitz's ideas, in Michael Handel, *Masters of War: Classical Strategic Thought*, 2nd Edition (London: Frank Cass, 1996), Chapter 12.
[27] Carl von Clausewitz, *On War*, translated and edited by Michael Howard and Peter Paret (Princeton, NJ: Princeton University Press, 1976), p. 117.
[28] Cairncross, *The Death of Distance*, p. 261.
[29] John Arquilla and David Ronfeldt, *The Advent of Netwar* (Santa Monica, CA: RAND, 1996).
[30] Hanna, 'Task Force XXI: The Army's Digital Experiment'.
[31] Jason Sherman, 'Digitization Decisions', *Armed Forces Journal International*, vol. 135, no. 3, October 1997.
[32] MacGregor, 'Future Battle: The Merging Levels of War', p. 42.
[33] Lieutenant-Colonel Dennis Murphy, 'Nontraditional Battlefield', *Military Review*, vol. 86, no. 6, November–December 1996, p. 16.
[34] David Alberts, 'The Future of Command and Control with DBK', in Johnson and Libicki (eds), *Dominant Battlespace Knowledge*, p. 80.
[35] Jablonsky, 'US Military Doctrine and the Revolution in Military Affairs'; Eliot Cohen, 'The Mystique of Air Power', *Foreign Affairs*, vol. 73, no. 1, January–February 1994.

**Chapter 5**

[1] Gladys Ganley, 'Power to the People via Personal Electronic Media', *The Washington Quarterly*, vol. 14, no. 2, Spring 1991, pp. 5–26.
[2] Joseph Nye and William Owen, 'America's Information Edge', *Foreign Affairs*, vol. 75, no. 2, March–April 1996. See also Martin Libicki, 'The Emerging Primacy of Information', *Orbis*, vol. 40, no. 2, Spring 1996, pp. 261–76.
[3] *Ibid.*, p. 24.
[4] Eliot Cohen, 'A Revolution in Warfare', *Foreign Affairs*, vol. 75, no. 2, March–April 1996, p. 53.
[5] See, for example, Paul Dibb, 'The Revolution in Military Affairs and Asian Security', paper prepared for the 39th IISS Annual Conference, Singapore, September 1997.
[6] National Defense Panel, 'Transforming Defense'.
[7] Loren Thompson, 'The Misconceived B-2 Debate', *Armed Forces Journal International*, vol. 134, no. 11, June 1997, pp. 38–40.
[8] 'The Future of Unmanned Aerial Vehicles', IISS, *Strategic Comments*, vol. 3, no. 10, December 1997.
[9] Michael Pillsbury (ed.), *Chinese Views of Future Warfare* (Washington DC: National Defense University, 1997).
[10] 'Assessing the Cruise Missile Threat', *Strategic Survey 1996/97* (Oxford: Oxford University Press for the IISS, 1997), pp. 16–30; Dennis Gormley, 'Hedging Against the Cruise-Missile Threat', *Survival*, vol. 40, no. 1, Spring 1998, pp. 92–111.
[11] William Keller and Janne E. Nolan, 'The Arms Trade: Business as Usual?', *Foreign Policy*, no. 109, Winter 1997–98, p. 123.

[12] Nye and Owen, 'America's Information Edge', p. 27.
[13] Libicki, 'DBK and its Consequences', p. 38.


## Conclusion

[1] Joint Chiefs of Staff, *Joint Vision 2010* (Washington DC: Department of Defense, 1996), p. 1.
[2] MacGregor, *Breaking the Phalanx*.
[3] Lovelace, *The Evolution of Military Affairs*.
[4] Christopher Bellamy, *Knights in White Armour* (London: Pimlico, 1997).
[5] Jennifer M. Taw and Alan Vick, 'From Sideshow to Center Stage: The Role of the Army and Air Force in Military Operations Other Than War', in Zalmay M. Khalizad and David A. Ochmanek (eds), *Strategy and Defense Planning for the 21st Century* (Santa Monica, CA: RAND, 1997), pp. 208–09.
[6] David A. Ochmanek and Steve T. Hosmer reach similar conclusions. See 'The Context for Defense Planning: The Environment, Strategy, and Missions', in *ibid.*, p. 64.
[7] Christopher Jon Lamb summarises the results of a Pentagon project on the RMA that looked at low-intensity conflict. See 'The Impact of Information Age Technologies on Operations Other Than War', in Pfalzgraff and Shultz (eds), *War in the Information Age*, pp. 247–77.
[8] Davis, Kugler and Hillestad, *Strategic Issues and Options for the Quadrennial Defense Review*.
[9] A. C. Bacevich, 'Preserving the Well-Bred Horse', *The National Interest*, no. 37, Autumn 1994, p. 48.
[10] Lovelace, *The Evolution of Military Affairs*, p. 62. The examples cited come from the Project 2025 study of 1991; see Alvin Bernstein et al., *Project 2025* (Washington DC: National Defense University, 1997).